USING ICT IN THE PRIMARY SCHOOL

USING ICT IN THE PRIMARY SCHOOL

Carol Elston

P·C·P

Paul Chapman
Publishing

First published 2007

Paul Chapman Publishing
A SAGE Publications Company
1 Oliver's Yard
55 City Road
London EC1Y 1SP

SAGE Publications Inc
2455 Teller Road
Thousand Oaks, California 91320

SAGE Publications India Pvt Ltd
B-42, Panchsheel Enclave
Post Box 4109
New Delhi 110 017

Library of Congress Control Number: 2006904386

A catalogue record for this book is available from the
British Library

ISBN-13 978-1-4129-3000-0
ISBN-13 978-1-4129-3001-7

Typeset by C&M Digitals (P) Ltd, Chennai, India
Printed in Great Britain by The Cromwell Press, Trowbridge Wiltshire
Printed on paper from sustainable resources

CONTENTS

ABOUT THE AUTHOR

Carol Elston is an established author with over 25 published educational titles and CD-ROMS. Her areas of interest span ICT in primary education through to Internet access for 'silver-surfers'.

The field of education has featured throughout Carol's career, from teaching IT in an educational environment through to commercial business training. Carol is the Director/owner of a successful training and development organisation; Change Associated Training Solutions (CATS). She also works as a freelance author currently writing NVQ units and working on a learning development research project at the University of Leeds. In her 'spare time' she is studying for an MA ICT and Education.

ACKNOWLEDGEMENTS

My thanks go to the many people who have supported me in the production of this book. I am particularly grateful to Mark Elston, Sue Moores, Janine Thornhill (HLTA, Moortown Primary School, Leeds), Keith Wass (Education Leeds) and Jenni Wilcock (ICT Co-ordinator, Kerr Mackie Primary School, Leeds).

INTRODUCTION

This book considers the role of Information and Communication Technology (ICT) within the context of primary education (ages 3 to 11).

In simple terms the book has just two aims:

❏ to provide teachers with the ICT knowledge they need to confidently teach ICT skills and use ICT to aid planning, preparation and assessment

❏ to look at ways in which ICT can successfully be applied and integrated into the curriculum.

Throughout, the emphasis is placed on the difference between learning ICT skills and applying ICT. The two need not be mutually exclusive and this is demonstrated by highlighting the benefits of integrating ICT within the curriculum and learning ICT skills 'on the job'. In some cases teachers are still approaching ICT as a stand-alone subject rather than appreciating that it is a tool to be used to enhance all areas of education and school life.

This book also concentrates on the effective use of ICT. At one end of the spectrum, ICT can be over-used in the classroom; technology is best used as a tool that can improve an activity or make a task easier, but it is certainly not always the answer. But then equally, ICT can be under-utilised; some teachers avoid ICT at all costs and their class can miss out on discovering the huge benefits that technology can bring. It is hoped that, after reading this book, teachers will have the knowledge and confidence to find a happy medium for the use of ICT, incorporating it whenever it adds value to their pupils' education.

How to use this book

This book is designed to be easily navigated and, as such, is divided into three distinct parts. There is a logical progression of information for those who like to read a book from start to finish. However, in general, readers are encouraged to dip in to the book as their needs dictate.

Part A provides background information designed to help the reader appreciate the current status of ICT within primary schools along with some of the history behind the journey. It begins by exposing ICT, taking away some of the mystique that still surrounds computer technologies. It then moves on to consider how ICT has developed within primary education through government initiatives and funding and the ways in which teachers have been equipped to deal with these changes.

Part B provides a practical guide to ICT including activities and guidance for teachers. Theory and exercises incorporate the full range of applications included within the ICT curriculum as well as the software required for professional activities such as preparation, assessment and general school administration.

Part C considers the specified learning areas for the Foundation Stage and the ICT Qualifications and Curriculum Authority (QCA) scheme of work for each year group within Key Stage 1 and Key Stage 2. Teachers are encouraged to 'benchmark' their new class against the expected levels of experience and understanding at the start of the year. They then consider the ICT skills required to meet the objectives for the year and devise practical ways in which the tasks can be integrated into the curriculum. This includes suggestions for exercises/activities for each year group.

Who is this book for?

This book is designed for educational professionals involved in teaching or supporting ICT within primary education. More specifically:

- ❑ Trainee teachers

- ❑ HLTAs and TAs (Teaching Assistants)

- ❑ Established teachers

- ❑ Supply teachers

- ❑ ICT Coordinators.

The responsibility for the effective use of ICT within a primary school goes beyond the classroom teacher. Teaching Assistants (TAs) and more specifically Higher Level Teaching Assistants (HLTAs) are playing an increasingly important part in the education of children at primary level. In some schools suitably trained HLTAs are delivering ICT lessons and including the use of ICT within other areas of the curriculum. In most schools Teaching Assistants support qualified teachers within the classroom. As ICT becomes increasingly embedded within the curriculum an understanding of ICT is essential if TAs are to provide a positive contribution.

In addition to the focus of ICT within the teaching context, ICT is also playing an increasingly important role in the management of primary schools. The majority of administrative systems are now computerised and channels of communication, both internal and external, require computer technology. A level of ICT expertise is essential for all those working within education.

This book is designed to provide something for all.

- ❑ For the ICT Coordinator it provides a reference and a training tool.

- ❑ For established and supply teachers it provides detailed teaching suggestions on a year-by-year basis, links to resources and step-by-step refresher sessions for software applications.

- ❑ For HLTAs and TAs it provides it all; a cover-to-cover read is recommended, if time permits.

- ❑ For trainee teachers it provides a useful reference during training and a trusted guide for those first few years in the classroom.

BACKGROUND INFORMATION

The first two chapters of this book are designed to set the scene and provide an overview for those new to ICT or new to primary education (or both).

The first chapter, 'ICT exposed', provides a brief overview of the world of computers and the associated technologies. One of the main aims of this book is to provide teachers with the ICT knowledge they need to confidently teach ICT skills. Without the basic knowledge and understanding of the technologies involved, a teacher or Teaching Assistant cannot be expected to confidently embrace ICT and use it within lessons or as tool for planning and preparation. This chapter endeavours to give confidence and is designed for those with limited or confused knowledge when it comes to computers and the associated technologies that make up ICT. The aim is to include enough information to provide a clear understanding without being too technical or delving too deeply into the subject. This simplified approach to ICT may not answer all the questions but it will provide a foundation that can be built upon through experience and further reading.

The second chapter, 'ICT in primary education', sets out to discover how ICT has developed to become an integral part of today's primary curriculum. This chapter is designed to provide an overview of ICT within the primary school environment. Initial sections set the scene by looking at the background to the development of ICT within primary schools with respect to government initiatives and funding incentives. Following sections discuss the integration of ICT within teaching as well as the wider use in planning, preparation and school administration systems. Consideration is given to the development and support requirements of teachers and training assistants. The final section provides a brief review of the assessment of ICT from the pupil perspective as well as external inspection by the Office for Standards in Education (Ofsted).

CHAPTER 1

ICT exposed

The following chapter looks at the many facets of ICT (a glossary of terms can be found in Appendix A). This includes an overview of the components of a personal computer, computer network and general IT equipment found within the school environment. The software used within primary education is discussed in Part B. And, of course, an overview of ICT in the twenty-first century would not be complete without considering the Internet and the many features it brings. As well as the positive impact the Internet has on our lives, the useful 'Internet dos and don'ts' on page 12 provides a reminder of the inherent dangers of the Internet and the steps that can be taken to keep children safe.

What exactly is ICT?

ICT stands for Information and Communication Technology and is not dissimilar to IT, Information Technology. The communication part was added relatively recently and has been adopted by educational establishments. Within industry and the corporate world it is still usually referred to as IT. There are literally thousands of definitions for IT and ICT but in the simplest form, IT can be defined as 'the technology used to manage information' and ICT defined as 'the technology used to manage information and aid communication'. In practice the two terms are interchangeable and refer to devices such as video recorders, telephones, calculators, electronic cash tills as well as computers.

In the context of the primary school classroom, ICT usually comprises:

- ❑ Computers (personal computers – PCs)
- ❑ Laptop computers
- ❑ Computer network
- ❑ Printers
- ❑ Scanners
- ❑ Video and DVD players

❑ Digital cameras (still and video)

❑ Voice recorders (tape and CD)

❑ Interactive whiteboards.

The following sections provide a brief overview of each of the listed technologies suggesting how they may be utilised in the classroom setting.

Computers

Although computers are just one type of technology it is true to say that they do make up the majority of a school's ICT equipment. A computer, often referred to as a personal computer or PC, is made up of a number of components. It will usually include the system unit, a screen (visual display unit – VDU), a keyboard, a disk or compact disc (CD) drive and a mouse. To be correct, the computer is really just the devices held within the casing of the system unit. The system unit houses the central processing unit (CPU), the part that does all the work, the 'brain' of the computer and storage units that hold information while being processed or waiting to be processed. The other devices – screen, keyboard, mouse, etc. – are needed to get information into and out of the computer. These 'add-on' devices are sometimes referred to as peripherals (devices that are on the periphery or perimeter).

Sometimes a PC will have additional peripherals such as a printer, scanner, speakers or digital camera. The devices that are used to put information into the computer such as the keyboard, the mouse or scanner are referred to as input devices. Devices that are used to get information out of the computer, for example a printer or speakers, are known as output devices. Some devices such as disk drives and CD or DVD (digital video/versatile disc) drives can be both input and output devices. Information can be loaded into the computer from a disk, CD or DVD and it can also be copied back onto the disk, CD or DVD at the end of a session (if the CD or DVD are read/write, meaning that they can be read and written to). Disk, CD and DVD drives are often built into the system unit as they are integral parts of the PC.

Collectively, the devices that 'make up' a PC are often referred to as computer hardware.

Schools vary in the way they utilise their computers. Some distribute the PCs throughout the school, placing a few in each classroom, whereas others set up an ICT suite. Depending on the quantity of PCs available, there may be scope for having both an ICT suite and PCs available in some or all classrooms.

In most schools PCs will also be found in the general office, library and the offices of staff with management responsibility.

Laptop computers

A laptop computer (sometimes referred to as a portable computer) is a compact device where the system unit and peripherals such as the screen, keyboard, mouse, speakers, disk, CD and DVD drives are all housed within the same unit. A laptop computer is lightweight and portable and ideal for those working in a number of locations.

It is the government's aim to ensure that all teachers are equipped with a laptop computer by 2006. The rationale is the expectation that teachers will use the laptop both at school and at home, increasing their experience and expertise. The laptop can also be used as a teaching aid in the classroom for one-to-one demonstration or linked to an interactive whiteboard for class sessions.

Computer network

A computer network is a number of computers linked together using cables. The main reason for linking PCs together is so that they can share resources. For example, individual PCs each need their own printer whereas a network of several computers can share the one printer. Networked computers can also share computer programs. Rather than loading the computer program (software) onto a number of individual PCs it can be loaded onto a special computer known as a network server. All the machines in the network can then access the software from the server.

Primary schools use network technology to enable them to share hardware and software as well as providing the opportunity for a number of children to access external resources concurrently. A school's network will usually be linked to the Internet and the Local Education Authority (LEA)'s intranet facilities.

Printers

Printers are used to produce a paper copy (hardcopy) of work created using the computer. This could, for instance, be a printout of a typed document, a picture, a photograph or a graph. There are different types of printers providing a range of quality and speed. The most popular types of printer are the laser and inkjet printers.

The laser printer uses a laser to produce an image on a rotating drum. The image is then transferred to paper by using an electric charge to deposit toner. Some new models of laser printer also serve as scanners, faxes and copiers.

One of the most affordable printers available today is the inkjet printer. In simple terms this printer works by placing small drops of ink onto the paper. The ink is transferred through nozzles that spray the ink directly onto the paper.

Within the classroom, printers are often used to produce a paper record of children's work, either for classroom displays or assessment.

Scanners

A scanner (flatbed scanner) is a device that converts visual information into digital data. The image is transferred to the computer where editing software provides the capability to alter the scanned information. Images can be manipulated in many ways; they can be resized, cropped, the colours changed, text can be added and the quality of the image can be enhanced. Text documents can also be scanned and then edited using Optical Character Recognition (OCR) software. Scanner prices now start at well under £50 for a bottom-of-the-range model making them affordable for school and home use.

Within a primary school a scanner can be used to scan children's work such as paintings, drawings and examples of handwriting. These can then form part of computerised documents such as reports or newsletters. The scanned work can also be included within web pages on the school's website or e-mailed to parents and carers.

Film and voice technologies

ICT provides the opportunity for children to experiment with a whole range of equipment including video and DVD players, digital cameras and voice recorders. Technology develops at a rapid pace and with each new advance the cost of the previous model falls substantially. Modern technologies are now an affordable option both in the home and at school. In the main, the DVD has superseded video, and traditional cameras are now being outsold by the digital variety. These new technologies have been designed to integrate with computer technology: digital photos can be loaded from the camera directly to the computer where they can be enhanced, manipulated and then sent to a printer; DVDs can be played via a DVD drive located in the system unit of the computer and watched on the computer screen. Computers can also be used to record voice and music.

The opportunities for using these technologies within the classroom are endless. Children as young as three can operate a digital camera and with help can print the photo. Older children will gain immense enjoyment through using video cameras and voice-recording equipment to record events and performances. When planning lessons it is so important to remember that ICT isn't just about computers.

Interactive whiteboards

Interactive (or electronic) whiteboards (IWBs) are the most recent addition to the primary classroom. In simple terms an interactive whiteboard is an erasable writing surface that interacts with a computer to capture writing electronically and enable interaction with a projected computer image. In order to work, the whiteboard needs to be attached to a multimedia projector and a computer. The multimedia projector connects to the VDU socket of the computer and projects the computer's image onto the interactive whiteboard. The interactive whiteboard then connects via a cable into the mouse socket of the computer and can be positioned at the front of the classroom so that all children have a clear view.

Interactive whiteboards work by either using a special pen or by finger touch. As the pen or finger is moved across the whiteboard the mouse cursor follows. Tapping the screen twice with a finger provides the same action as double-clicking the mouse. These finger touch whiteboards are ideal for primary schools where even the youngest children can move their finger across the whiteboard and interact with the computer program.

An interactive whiteboard comes with software that enables it to be used as a copyboard. Teachers and children can write or draw on the whiteboard with their finger or the pens provided and save the image to the computer. These images can then be printed or e-mailed. The software that comes with interactive whiteboards also has built-in OCR. This means that the computer will recognise the handwriting on the whiteboard and turn it into computer text.

A recent report from the University of Newcastle (Embedding ICT, 2005) concluded that the introduction of IWBs has had a real impact on the primary classroom. The response from both the teachers and the pupils involved in the project was overwhelmingly positive. Most (if not all) schools now have at least one IWB with some schools installing them in every classroom. In the main, teachers and children have readily adapted to this new technology, realising the benefits that electronic whiteboards can bring to a classroom session. Training sessions for teachers has greatly helped with the integration, providing the skills to operate the boards as well identifying potential uses such as:

- ❑ writing over the top of displayed information to highlight and annotate points

- ❑ surfing the Internet and displaying websites which the entire class are able to see

❑ enabling children to add their contribution to the discussion by writing directly on the whiteboard

❑ demonstrating ICT work before the children move to the ICT suite for a session

❑ displaying movie files or DVDs from the PC.

The Internet

The Internet has had a huge impact on teaching, providing access to information and resources. Conceived in the USA in the late 1960s, the Internet has grown to be a vast, worldwide network of computers that are linked together, providing a means of communicating and sharing information. Until quite recently most of the information was in plain text with reams of programming code in between. In 1989 Tim Berners-Lee came up with the idea of linking pages of information, making it easy to jump to a document of interest. It wasn't long before businesses began to make software to present these pages and the links between them in an attractive way that was easy to use; this was the beginning of the World Wide Web.

It is estimated that about 30 million people in the UK and about 600 million worldwide now use the Internet to search for information and send e-mails. The World Wide Web is the part of the Internet that most people use. It is made up of billions of linked web pages that contain pictures, text, sounds and animations. The Internet has many uses; here are some of the more popular applications:

❑ Keeping in touch with friends and family around the world using e-mail.

❑ Copying files to a PC (downloading music and video files).

❑ Keeping up to date with the latest news from around the world.

❑ Accessing the billions of pages of information held on the World Wide Web.

❑ Searching for bargains and buying goods and services.

❑ Creating websites.

No one owns the Internet as such. Some large organisations own the computers and cables that make up the Internet but no single person owns all the information stored in the web pages. Equally, anyone can put information on the Internet and that is why there are billions of pages available. No one checks that the information on the Internet is correct or true so it is important to always double check facts by looking at more than one website or cross-checking using books or other sources of information.

Connecting to the Internet

Connecting to the Internet is known as going online. Going online requires a computer, a means of physically connecting to the Internet and the services of an Internet Services Provider (ISP) to enable access to the many networks that make up the Internet.

Computers can be physically connected to the Internet in a number of ways, the most popular method being via a telephone line (dial-up). Because computers and telephone lines generally don't speak the same language, a special piece of equipment is needed to do this. This equipment is called a modulator demodulator (MODEM). Computers store information as a sequence of digits 1 and 0 (digital format) and this needs to be converted to electrical voltages (analogue format) before it travels down the telephone line. It then needs to be converted back into digital format at the other end so that the receiving computer can read it. Most computers these days come with a built-in MODEM and are referred to as 'Internet ready'.

Connecting to the Internet using a MODEM can be slow and there is the added inconvenience of not being able to use the telephone to make or receive calls at the same time. Because of these problems, people are moving to Broadband, a high-speed Internet connection, typically ten times faster than dial-up Internet. With Broadband, information is transferred at a fast rate and the telephone can still be used when online. When speaking on the phone only a small part of the capacity of the telephone cable or line is used; Broadband technologies make use of this spare capacity.

Once physically connected to the Internet it is necessary to invest in the services of an ISP. Broadly speaking, ISPs invest in and manage extensive computer networks and provide links to networks across the world. The costs and services on offer can differ but in general an ISP provides access to the World Wide Web, use of e-mail, space for a website and access to newsgroups and chatrooms.

For further information on accessing the World Wide Web and e-mail, see Chapter 4.

Using the Internet in school

Computers and the Internet are now a part of children's everyday life and while the Internet is undoubtedly of great use to children, it also has a darker side. There are two main sources of danger to children: they could come across unsuitable sites while surfing the Internet, and/or they could 'meet' undesirable characters through e-mail contact or in chatrooms.

A chatroom is a collection of people sending messages to each other via the Internet. The conversations happen in 'real time' so, unlike e-mail, there is no time delay before getting a response to a message. It is widely acknowledged that some adult sexual predators use chatrooms to 'groom' young people and attempt to arrange face-to-face meetings. It is important to educate children, from an early age, about safe online practices. The Net Smart rules set out by the NCH (formally known as the National Children's Home) can provide a good starting point for talking about the potential dangers. There are five things that a child should never do and six things that he or she should always do (see over for a photocopiable list of these Internet 'dos and don'ts').

Internet dos and don'ts

✗ Never tell anyone you meet on the Internet your home address, your telephone number or your school's name, unless your parent or carer specifically gives you permission.

✗ Never send anyone your picture, credit-card or bank details, without first checking with your parent or carer.

✗ Never arrange to meet anyone unless your parent or carer goes with you and you meet in a public place. People you contact online are not always who they seem, even people who become pen friends or 'keypals'. People don't always tell the truth online – no one can see them.

✗ Never open attachments to e-mails unless they come from someone you already know and trust. They could contain viruses or other programs which would destroy all the information and software on your computer.

✗ Never respond to nasty or suggestive messages. Always tell your parent or carer if you get such messages or if you see rude pictures while online and report them to your Internet Service Provider.

✓ Always keep your password to yourself, do not share it with anyone.

✓ Always check with your parent or carer that it is okay to be in a chatroom.

✓ Always be very careful in chatrooms. Even if a chatroom says it is only for children, there's no way at the moment to tell if everyone there really is a child. It might be an adult or an older child trying to trick you.

✓ Always get out of a chatroom if someone says or writes something which makes you feel uncomfortable or worried. Make sure you tell your parent or carer.

✓ Always be yourself and do not pretend to be anyone or anything you are not.

✓ Always stay away from sites that say they are for people over 18 only. The warnings are there to protect you. Adult sites can sometimes cost a lot more on your phone bill too.

Photocopiable: Using Ict in the Primary School
Paul Chapman Publishing 2007 © Carol Elston

Search engines and filters for children

Educational networks usually include filters to make sure that unsuitable information cannot be accessed within the school environment, however, children will use the Internet in other locations and it is important to ensure that they are aware of search facilities that do afford some degree of protection. Search engines such as Google, Yahoo and MSN do not censor information although they do aim to block pages that contain text or images that are illegal. Search engines specifically designed for children, however, do filter out web pages considered to be unsuitable for a child either due to the nature or the complexity of the material. This can afford a degree of protection but the choice of search engine cannot be monitored if a child is surfing the Net unsupervised.

The more popular search engines for children are probably Yahooligans, Ask for Kids and KidsClick! These are all suitable for younger children although they can be restrictive. For more information on using search engines, see Chapter 4.

The next level of protection is the Internet Filter. Filtering software controls the sites that can be accessed regardless of the search engine used. The majority of filters use a combination of methods to prevent access to objectionable material, including using a list of banned sites, banning sites that contain specified keywords and blocking pages that contain barred words or phrases. Filters such as AOL and Net Nanny have received a great deal of publicity through television advertising campaigns.

📖 References and useful websites

Embedding ICT, 2005 – *Embedding ICT in the Literacy and Numeracy Strategies*, April 2005, University of Newcastle – report of the effectiveness of electronic whiteboards:

www.becta.org.uk/page-documents/research/univ-newcastle-evaluation-whiteboards.pdf

AOL	www.aol.com
Ask for Kids	www.askforkids.com
KidsClick!	www.kidsclick.com
NCH	www.nchafc.org.uk
Net Nanny	www.netnanny.com
Yahooligans	www.yahooligans.yahoo.com

CHAPTER 2

ICT in primary education

Before looking at ICT in primary schools today, this chapter briefly considers the steps taken by the government to introduce and develop ICT within schools since the mid – 1980s.

Computer technology has been available within schools for many years, certainly from the days of the Acorn computers back in the 1980s. However, it wasn't until 1988, as a result of the Education Reform Act, that a formal curriculum was defined for each subject, including Information Technology (IT). The UK was one of the first countries to define a national curriculum for 5- to 16-year-olds, specifying four key stages identified by school years and pupil ages. The content of the curriculum was developed as a programme of study covering the minimum statutory requirement for knowledge, understanding and skills. The expected standards of student performance at each key stage were specified through attainment targets.

The curriculum was reviewed in 1995 and the requirements for IT within the National Curriculum (1995) were stated as being 'an ability to use effectively IT tools and information sources to analyse, process and present information, and to model, measure and control external events.' This update to the curriculum set the wheels in motion and the subsequent government initiatives were instrumental in raising the profile of IT within primary schools. The transition to integrate IT into primary education was certainly made easier by three government initiatives: the introduction of the National Grid for Learning; funding for the purchasing of up-to-date equipment; and IT training for teaching and support staff. These initiatives were introduced from 1997 but it wasn't until 2000 that the term ICT entered the primary educational vocabulary. The change from IT to ICT was introduced as part of the National Curriculum for schools in England (2000) to reflect the growing importance of communication when considering Information Technology.

The evolution of ICT within primary education has had a mixed reception. Excitement to absolute dread covers the range of emotions experienced by primary school teachers with many needing to retrain to keep ahead of computer savvy pupils raised in homes where a PC is as common as a TV. Although ICT is still not embraced by all it is generally the view that the measures taken by the government over the past few years have helped to equip primary schools with the resources and expertise to integrate ICT into the National Curriculum.

Funding for ICT

The world of ICT can be extremely frustrating wherever you work and primary schools are no exception. There are never enough PCs, the PCs don't work, the Internet connection is slow or non-existent, the software doesn't do what you thought it did or, the old favourite, the printer doesn't work. Believe it or not, things are not as bad as they used to be. Those teaching in the 1990s will probably have seen huge improvements to the ICT facilities available within schools, but with many primary schools there is still a long way to go. In order to fully understand the development of ICT within primary education it is important to look at the funding issues, past, present and future.

The history of ICT funding

In 1997, when the Labour government came to power, the quality and quantity of ICT resources within schools was poor. One of the first steps to address this was the development of the National Grid for Learning (NGfL). The NGfL is designed to make quality educational resources available to all those working within education. It links to the Internet and provides access to websites that contain information and resources that have been selected for quality and accuracy. Once this facility was in place it was soon apparent that many schools didn't have adequate technology to access the resources. With many computers being over five years old and without adequate Internet access, this new resource could not be utilised to its full potential. To address this issue the government introduced the first wave of funding to equip schools with up-to-date computer equipment. The money was held in the Standards Fund, a centrally controlled pot of money that is allocated to schools via LEAs who prepare bids to central government.

With the introduction of this new equipment to schools it was soon realised that there was an additional need, training for teachers. To address this, the New Opportunities Fund (NOF) ICT Training Initiative was set up using funds from the Heritage Lottery. Training started in April 1999 and ran for a three-year period. During this time £230 million was made available by NOF for training purposes with another £50 million being spent on the digitisation of educational and learning materials. Approved commercial training providers where used to facilitate this training with courses designed to develop the ICT skills of existing teachers. During this period, Initial Teacher Training (ITT) programmes were also enhanced to develop the skills of trainee teachers, assuring adequate ICT knowledge for both existing and future teachers.

How has this funding improved ICT within primary schools?

Without a doubt the investment in technology and training has catapulted primary schools into the twenty-first century; however, ICT is an ever-evolving discipline leaving no room for complacency.

A recent report (ICT in Schools Survey, 2004) highlights some interesting statistics.

- ❑ The mean expenditure for primary schools on ICT increased from £3,600 per annum in 1998 to £14,700 in 2004.

- ❑ The mean number of computers in primary schools increased from 13.3 in 1998 to 31.6 in 2004.

❑ The mean number of pupils per computer in primary schools decreased from 17.6 in 1998 to 7.5 (1 computer for every 7.5 pupils) in 2004.

❑ The percentage of teaching staff confident in using computers rose from 65% in 1998 to 85% in 2004.

Teaching ICT in primary schools

The majority of primary schools are now reasonably equipped for ICT with teachers feeling confident and adequately trained in its use. With this confidence and familiarity has come the capacity for reflection and innovation. Teachers are now looking for new ways to develop the ICT skills of their pupils. Until recently the structure for teaching ICT has been fairly rigid with the majority of schools adopting defined schemes of work as a means of applying the curriculum. In many cases schools have taught ICT as an independent subject, often finding difficulty in covering all the topics within the time available. However, there have been recent initiatives designed to encourage innovation by empowering primary schools to take control of their curriculum. It is hoped that by taking more control, schools will find ways to truly integrate ICT into the curriculum whether adopting defined schemes of work or designing their own schemes that reflect the aims of the National Curriculum.

The National Curriculum

The National Curriculum is the key document for defining how to teach a subject within a primary school. All maintained schools use this framework to ensure a consistency in teaching and learning. There are two broad aims:

■ to promote the spiritual, moral, cultural, mental and physical development of pupils at the school and of society

■ to prepare pupils at the school for the opportunities, responsibilities and experiences of adult life.

The National Curriculum states the subjects that must be taught at each key stage, defining those subjects that are core and those considered non-core. It details the knowledge, skills and understanding required for each subject and sets targets enabling teachers to measure progress. Working within these guidelines, schools are encouraged to organise teaching in a way that best meets the needs of their pupils. At Key Stage 1 and Key Stage 2, Maths, English, Welsh* and Science are considered to be National Curriculum core subjects (*in Welsh schools only) whereas ICT falls under the heading of National Curriculum non-core foundation subject.

The National Curriculum is reviewed regularly and changes are made to reflect new and improved methods of learning. Between reviews, the government provides new initiatives in the form of strategies.

Strategy for primary schools
Since the overhaul of the National Curriculum in 2000, the Secretary of State has launched an *Excellence and Enjoyment* strategy aimed at empowering primary schools to take control of their curriculum, allowing them to be 'more innovative and to develop their own character' (A Strategy

for Primary Schools, 2003). The aim is to inject fun and enthusiasm into learning, providing scope to find new and interesting ways to teach areas of the curriculum. This 'loosening' of the curriculum can be seen as a way of encouraging the integration of ICT into both core and non-core subjects by introducing interactive and participative learning.

The strategy also aims to encourage schools to work together to share and develop good practice as well as working in partnership with parents/carers and forging wider links within the local community. The Extended Schools agenda will also promote this cooperative approach by working towards a situation where 'networks' of schools make provision for childcare from 8 a.m. to 6 p.m. as well as providing access to a range of children's services. By the year 2010, we should see a situation where schools are working together in clusters to provide these services, which will also provide opportunity for the sharing of ICT resources and expertise.

Five Year Strategy for Children and Learners

The Department for Education and Skills (DfES) has defined its Five Year Strategy for Children and Learners (Five Year Strategy, 2004). The report provides the following assurances for the next five years:

- *we will help primary schools develop and maintain their ICT infrastructure,*

- *we will ensure it is used effectively to improve teaching practice through the 'Primary Strategy',*

- *all primary schools will have broadband by 2006,*

- *we expect to see an increasing number of interactive whiteboards in primary schools,*

- *we expect to see more teachers having access to laptops,*

- *we expect to see an increasingly sophisticated use of ICT to support learning and management systems.*

The National Curriculum for ICT

ICT is a National Curriculum non-core foundation subject that became statutory from August 2000. The National Curriculum for ICT states:

Pupils should be given opportunities to apply and develop their ICT capability through the use of ICT tools to support their learning in all subjects (at key stage 1, there are no statutory requirements to teach the use of ICT in the programmes of study for the non-core foundation subjects. Teachers should use their judgement to decide where it is appropriate to teach the use of ICT across these subjects at key stage 1. At other key stages, there are statutory requirements to use ICT in all subjects, except physical education).

Pupils should be given opportunities to support their work by being taught to:

☐ *find things out from a variety of sources, selecting and synthesising the information to meet their needs and developing an ability to question its accuracy, bias and plausibility*

☐ *develop their ideas using ICT tools to amend and refine their work and enhance its quality and accuracy*

☐ *exchange and share information, both directly and through electronic media*

☐ *review, modify and evaluate their work, reflecting critically on its quality, as it progresses.*

The Qualifications and Curriculum Authority

The Qualifications and Curriculum Authority (QCA) was created in 1997 with a remit to develop a coherent national framework for all academic and vocational qualifications. Within primary education it does this by translating the National Curriculum into schemes of work for each year within Key Stage 1 and Key Stage 2. Although not compulsory, many schools use the QCA schemes of work to plan the curriculum and assess pupil achievement.

With the 'loosening' of the curriculum from 2006, more schools may choose to develop their own schemes of work. However, in practice, schools are likely to decide that they do not have the time or resources to re-invent the wheel. For many schools the QCA schemes provide an adequate structure for designing lesson plans coupled with the fact that external teaching resources are often based on the QCA schemes. In the short term at least, it is envisaged that many schools will still adopt the QCA schemes of work. When considering ICT, it is anticipated that schools, if not already doing so, will start to integrate the learning points into other areas of the curriculum rather than treating ICT as a stand-alone subject.

The individual QCA schemes of work for each school year are documented within Chapter 10 (Key Stage 1) and Chapter 11 (Key Stage 2) with suggestions for ways in which the areas of learning can be integrated throughout the curriculum.

Using ICT within a primary school

Electronic registers, communication via e-mail, pupil databases are just a few of the systems in place in the majority of schools. Most of the information provided by LEAs is sent as electronic documents via e-mail or is downloaded from the Internet. With the provision of laptop computers teachers are expected to actively develop their ICT skills both at work and at home. For some this is second nature but for others it can be daunting and they may need encouragement to experiment and persevere.

Any reticence is gradually being replaced with enthusiasm as teaching staff realise the benefits that ICT can bring to their working life, but some staff are regrettably going to find that they are dragged along as schools increasing rely on computerised administration systems.

Effective use of ICT within a school can save time, money and resources, all good reasons for investing in the hardware, software and the training needed to ensure that systems run smoothly. Another reason for moving forward with technology is the expectations of stakeholders. A whole range of stakeholders and community members, including parents/carers, school governors and visiting educational professionals, expect a school to make the optimum use of technology. The major part of a school's financial budget is made up of monies received based on pupil numbers. Attracting pupils to a school is one of the major concerns for head teachers and governing bodies. Schools often need to compete to secure sufficient children, especially primary schools at a time when the birth rate has been falling.

It is important that a school demonstrates its ICT ability and it can easily do so in a few simple yet effective ways:

- ❑ The use of displays in the classrooms and general areas, demonstrating the use of ICT within the curriculum.

- ❑ A school website, preferably developed and managed internally with input from all stakeholders including pupils.

- ❑ The option for school notices and documents to be sent to parents/carers via email.

- ❑ An up-to-date pupil database including emergency and contact data.

- ❑ Open days where stakeholders are actively encouraged to view and use ICT facilities.

- ❑ Regular updates to stakeholders on enhancements and additions to the ICT capability of the school.

- ❑ The celebration of success (in all areas including ICT).

Development and support for those teaching ICT

The professional standards for Qualified Teacher Status (QTS) state that teachers should know how to use ICT effectively, both to teach their subject and to support their wider professional role. The revised draft standard (January 2006) gives the same message; teachers should know how to use skills in literacy, numeracy and ICT to underpin their teaching and support their wider professional activities. Teachers are expected to use ICT as a learning tool but also to recognise the importance of ICT in planning, assessment and classroom management. ITT programmes reflect this by encouraging trainees to use ICT with discrimination and appropriately when both planning and delivering lessons. The emphasis in the classroom is on using ICT only where it adds value to a pupil's learning experience. The standards for QTS and practice skills tests can be found on the Training and Development Agency (TDA) website.

Newly Qualified Teachers (NQTs) will have a good grasp of ICT, enabling them to effectively integrate it into lessons as well as use it for lesson planning and administrative activities. More established teaching staff and TAs may find that they have skill gaps within their ICT knowledge. Although the initial NOF training for teachers came to an end a few years ago, most schools have continued to provide ICT development for teachers and support staff through In Service Training (INSET). The aim is to build the confidence of existing teachers and support staff through exposure to a range of software and hardware. The recent introduction of laptop computers and interactive whiteboards has in most cases been coupled with training sessions either through the providers of the equipment, external training providers or by cascade training via the ICT Coordinator or other experienced member of staff.

 Recognising a need for self-development is half the battle. The majority of schools are keen to develop the ICT skills of their staff whether through formal training, mentoring or self-development.

ICT training and development is not only restricted to qualified teachers, with the introduction of Planning, Preparation and Assessment (PPA) time for teaching staff, many primary schools are looking to utilise the ICT expertise and skills of HLTAs within the classroom.

From September 2005 all teaching staff are entitled to spend 10 per cent of their timetabled classroom commitment time away from the classroom carrying out planning, preparation or assessment activities. This has resulted in major issues with resourcing, resulting in some schools recruiting additional qualified teaching staff. Many schools, however, have not had available funds to recruit more staff and have had to come up with more innovative solutions. A popular route is to capitalise on the skills of existing support staff, particularly those with specific interests such as music, drama and ICT. In some schools HLTAs with ICT expertise have been given appropriate training and development to enable them to confidently facilitate ICT lessons, thus 'freeing up' teachers for PPA time.

Support from the ICT Coordinator

The majority of primary schools have appointed an ICT Coordinator. This is an important and valued role providing support, advice and cohesion. The role of the ICT Coordinator will differ from school to school depending on the size of the school, the experience of the Coordinator and the experience of the teaching and support staff. In general the Coordinator will be involved in identifying ICT-related areas for inclusion within the School Development Plan and then taking the responsibility to action or manage any identified initiatives. The ICT Coordinator also acts as a role model, using ICT skills effectively within their teaching and supporting activities.

Assessment of ICT

Pupil assessment

The standards and methodology for assessing pupil achievement are equally relevant to ICT as to any other subject within the curriculum. However, measuring achievement within ICT shares some of the challenges found with subjects such as PE; it is relatively straightforward to observe and record progress but it is more difficult providing evidence.

The use of ICT often requires a complex process with the end result not always providing an accurate reflection of the processes and effort required. Take, for example, a word-processed document; the printed end result does not necessarily reflect the editing work or formatting skills required to complete the task. Equally a graph produced as part of a science experiment may not show the time and effort involved in positioning the labels or refining the scale.

The most effective way to assess ICT is by observation. This is particularly relevant for collaborative work where children work in pairs or small groups in order to complete a task. Without observing the process it is difficult to assess the input that individual children have had to the end product. Ideally an ICT assessment task should simply be an activity within a curriculum topic involving the use of ICT, enabling the teacher to observe and note how the pupils coped with the ICT.

External assessment of ICT

Formal external assessment of primary education is the responsibility of Ofsted. The British Educational Communications and Technology Agency (Becta) website provides the following advice and guidance for Ofsted Inspectors when considering ICT within schools (Advice for Ofsted inspectors from Becta, 2005).

If you are leading the inspection of ICT you will need to ask the following questions:

- ❑ *What is the school's approach to teaching ICT, in particular, is it taught in timetabled ICT lessons or integrated into other subjects?*

- ❑ *Where and when is ICT taking place that is not shown on the class timetables?*

- ❑ *What extra-curricular opportunities are there for you to observe ICT being taught?*

- ❑ *What is the location and availability of all educational computers and other ICT resources?*

ACTIVITY

It is worth considering these questions and preparing your answers and evidence before an inspection. In addition, use the following checklist as a starting point for your Ofsted preparation. Consider your responsibilities for ICT in a teaching context as well as your utilisation of ICT within the general school environment:

⇨ Find a copy of your school's last Ofsted report and highlight all the references to ICT.

⇨ Make a list of all the areas that received positive feedback and make sure that you can show (gather evidence) that these areas are still as good if not better.

⇨ Make a list of the areas needing improvement and collect evidence to illustrate improvement or action plans to show those areas still needing attention.

⇨ Make sure you know your facts; what is the computer to pupil ratio within the school, what computers do you have, what software are you using?

⇨ What other ICT tools do you use (digital cameras, tape recorders, calculators, etc.)?

⇨ Provide evidence that ICT is used cross curricula.

⇨ Where are the computers located?

⇨ How do you assess pupils' ICT development?

⇨ Who is the ICT Coordinator, what is their role?

⇨ How is your ICT teaching monitored and assessed?

⇨ What ICT training have you received?

Make sure that your classroom displays clearly demonstrate the use of ICT within a variety of subjects. Have at hand examples of work involving a range of ICT devices (computer, digital camera, voice recorder).

References and useful websites

ICT in Schools Survey, 2004 – Findings from a survey conducted in Spring 2004. A report to the DfES by Gillian Prior and Louise Hall, TNS Social. Download a copy from www.teachernet.gov.uk/wholeschool/ictis/research/

A Strategy for Primary Schools, 2003 – Copies of *Excellence and Enjoyment: A Strategy for Primary Schools* have been distributed to all primary schools. To receive a copy e-mail primary.document@dfes.gsi.gov.uk

Five Year Strategy, 2004 – DfES Five Year Strategy for Children and Learners: www.dfes.gov.uk/publications/5yearstrategy/

Advice for Ofsted inspectors from Becta, 2005 – Ofsted inspection of ICT as a National Curriculum subject: www.becta.org.uk/corporate/corporate.cfm?section=1&id=2001

Becta's schools' website	www.becta.org.uk/Schools
Curriculum Online	www.curriculumonline.gov.uk
DfES and TTA standards for HLTAs	www.tda.gov.uk/teachers/currentconsultations/professionalstandards/
National Curriculum online	www.nc.uk.net
National Curriculum Wales	www.new.wales.gov.uk/topics/and education skills/?lang=en
National Curriculum Scotland	www.ltscotland.org.uk
National Curriculum Northern Ireland	www.ccea.org.uk
Practice skills tests	www.tda.gov.uk/skillstests/practicematerials.aspx
Professional standards	www.hlta.gov.uk/php/read.php?articleid=1385&sectionid=182
Qualifications and Curriculum Authority	www.qca.org.uk
Training and Development Agency	www.tda.gov.uk

GETTING TO GRIPS WITH ICT

This part is designed to provide an overview of the applications that are considered essential when meeting the ICT curriculum requirements for primary education. Broadly, these fall into the following categories:

- ❑ Operating system

- ❑ Internet and E-mail

- ❑ Text: Word processing and presentation

- ❑ Data: Spreadsheet, database and datalogging

- ❑ Creative: Graphics and music

- ❑ Control

Unfortunately, the scope of this book makes it impossible to look at these applications in detail; each affords a book in its own right. As a compromise, the following chapters attempt to provide a starting point and a suggested route forward. The approach is based on the supposition that those working within schools have two very different needs when it comes to computer software: they have a professional need and a teaching need. It is assumed that for professional applications such as assessments, preparation and administration (and home use), the Microsoft Office Suite will provide the most widely used applications, whereas a range of applications specifically designed for primary education will be utilised for teaching ICT. There are a host of excellent applications designed for this stage of education and this book will consider just a few of the more popular ones (for illustration purposes). Everyone has their own particular favourites but in most cases the functionality is similar and examples can easily be translated.

The content and order of the chapters has proved a challenge. It is difficult to know how best to group the applications as in many cases computer packages integrate a range of applications. However, a decision had to be made and the applications have been grouped based on their predominance for handling text or data and their use for creative or control activities. A brief overview is given with emphasis on professional use and the relevance within primary education.

Suggested activities

Each chapter is interspersed with suggested activities aimed to help the reader become familiar with their PC and software. Within some of these activities instructions involve the use of the terms listed on the following page.

Glossary of ICT-related terms

Point	Move the mouse so that the cursor on the screen is pointing to a specified object
Left-click	Click the left mouse button
Right-click	Click the right mouse button
Click	Click the left mouse button
Double-click	Click the specified mouse button twice in short succession
Access a menu	Click on the specified menu on the menu bar at the top of the screen
Select an option	Click on the specified option
Hover	Move the mouse over a specified object
Drag and drop	Point to the object, hold down the left mouse button, drag the object by moving the mouse and release the mouse button to place (drop) the object in the new position

Within some tasks there are prompts to 'find out'. These comments apply to settings or procedures that may differ between establishments.

Practise what you preach

Before you launch into this part it is important to remember that, like any other tool, ICT becomes much easier to use with practice. As with any other area of instruction, the more confident the teacher is with the topic the less stressful the teaching experience. Add some passion into the equation and the lesson can be a relaxing and enjoyable experience for all. Although not suggesting that teachers necessarily need to be passionate about ICT in order to deliver a valuable session, a belief in it as an effective tool is essential. It's the old adage of practise what you preach; if a teacher does not actively embrace ICT as a tool in their own life it is difficult to then 'sell it' to others. Children can spot a technophobe at twenty paces and will take huge delight it demonstrating their superior knowledge. Keeping one step ahead of a class is one way to survive but it will prove to be a stressful path to follow.

ICT development

A school is a place of lifelong learning; education is forever evolving and skills need constant updating. ICT is just one area of self-development and the support of colleagues and the ICT Coordinator is essential if staff are going to provide the best provision for children. In addition to the resources available via the Internet, there are a host of books available on all the popular computer applications. These books differ in style and approach and it is worth spending some time scouring the bookshops to find a book that suits your learning style. Book in hand, invest the time in working through the suggested activities until you gain the confidence to use the application both at home and at school.

Getting started

This chapter provides an overview of Microsoft Windows and those areas of functionality that are common to the programs within the Microsoft Office Suite. The MS Office programs have a common interface; that is, each program within the suite has a similar look and feel as well as having many of the same functions. For instance, the method of opening, saving and printing a document is the same in all the programs; the structure and the items on the menus are similar if not identical. Once familiar with one of the programs within the suite it becomes easier to use the others.

Microsoft Windows

The operating system is the most important program that runs on a computer; it is needed to run all the other programs. The operating system performs the basic tasks including recognising input from the keyboard, sending output to the screen, keeping track of files and directories on the hard disk, and controlling peripheral devices such as disk/CD drives and printers.

It is estimated that around 90% of all personal computers use Microsoft Windows as the operating system. Of the remaining 10%, the majority are Macintosh computers using the Macintosh operating system.

Windows is a GUI-style operating system; it provides a graphical user interface (GUI) to help the user manage their tasks. This simply means that Windows uses pictures (icons) and menus to help the user access programs, control peripherals and manage files; these are often referred to as housekeeping tasks. This chapter concentrates on the basic features of Microsoft Windows XP. Those using PCs that run earlier versions of Windows or alternative operating systems will find that the functionality is similar.

When a computer is turned on, a 'boot program' automatically loads the operating system. This is known as booting up the computer. There is a short delay while Windows checks to see what peripheral devices are attached to the PC and then it presents a welcome screen asking the user to select their username and in some cases enter a password. This feature is useful if a number of people are using the same PC; their personalised desktop and settings can be stored and loaded each time they log on. Once the user's settings are installed a blue screen, known as the

Windows desktop, is displayed (earlier versions of Windows may not display the welcome screen).

Windows is so named because it works by managing a series of windows. Multiple windows can be opened from the desktop. For example, if a user is producing a report that needs the features of both a word processor and a spreadsheet program, both applications can be open at the same time, in different windows. It is then possible for the user to switch between the two applications. It is also possible to open multiple files within an application with each file being displayed in a separate window. Again, Windows enables the user to switch back and forward between these windows when working on several documents concurrently. This approach provides flexibility and removes the inconvenience of having to close a file or application in order to open another one.

The Windows desktop

The Windows desktop will usually display a number of buttons on the left-hand side. These are known as icons and provide shortcuts for loading applications that are used frequently. The range of icons available on a PC will depend on the software loaded onto the hard disk of the computer and the shortcuts that have been set up. If Windows has been newly installed on the PC the only icon will be the **Recycle bin** icon. The **Taskbar** is generally located at the bottom of the screen although it can be moved to any other edge of the desktop.

Getting familiar with your desktop

⇨ Turn on your computer; notice the information that is displayed on the screen while Windows is loading.

⇨ If necessary log on to Windows to load your personal settings (if using a network, you may also need to log onto the network).

⇨ Look at the selection of icons displayed on your desktop. Do you know what they are shortcuts for? If not, find out. If you never use an icon, you can delete it (tidy up your desktop). Point to the icon and right-click. Select the **Delete** option. This will delete the shortcut icon; it does not remove the program.

⇨ Hover over the icons on the **Taskbar** to find out what programs are running in the background. If you are not sure what these programs do, find out.

⇨ Hover over the clock to see the date. Check that the date and time are correct (if incorrect, make a note to change later).

The Windows desktop (reproduced courtesy of Microsoft – www.microsoft.com)

Desktop options

⇨ Left-click the **Start** button. Hover over each option to find out what it does.

⇨ Click on the **My computer** option to find out more about your computer – its hard disk, removable storage and file storage. Click on the cross at the top right-hand corner of the window to close this window.

⇨ Click on the **Start** button then select the **Control panel** option. Left-click on the **Printers and faxes** option to find out if your PC is set up to access any printers. Close the window.

Customising the appearance and functionality of your computer

⇨ Left-click the **Start** button. Click on the **Control panel** option. This is where you can change many aspects of your computer.

⇨ If the date or time displayed on the **Taskbar** needs changing, double-click on the **Date and time** option, make the changes and click **OK**.

⇨ Double-click on the **Display** option and click on the **Desktop** tab to change the background of your desktop. Click on some of the options until you find a picture that is suitable. Alternatively, if you have any photos stored on your PC, click on the **Browse** button and locate a photo that you would like to appear as a background for your desktop. Once you have selected a background (from the list or from your photos) click **OK** to confirm.

⇨ Come back to the **Control panel** options and explore more as your experience increases.

Working with windows

Each window has three control buttons located at the top right-hand corner of the window.

Minimise – The **Minimise** button on the left 'shrinks' a window so that it appears as an icon on the **Taskbar** at the bottom of the page.

Restore/Maximise – The middle button displays as either the **Restore** or **Maximise** button. If displayed as shown, clicking on the button will 'restore' the window back to a size where the desktop/other open applications are visible. If the icon displays as just one square, it indicates that clicking on the button will 'maximise' the window so that it occupies as much space on the screen as it can.

Close – Clicking on the **Close** button will close that particular window or application.

Working with applications

Windows is just the tool that helps you manage your computer and access the applications you need for work or recreation. Once you have got to grips with Windows the next stage is to open and use an application. There are a couple of ways to do this from the desktop; the simplest method is to double-click the left mouse button when pointing to the application's shortcut icon. If the application does not have a shortcut icon displayed, the program can be selected from the **All programs** option on the **Start** menu.

The applications within the MS Suite all have a similar look and feel. At the top of every window there is a menu bar and a toolbar. The toolbar contains icons that act as shortcuts for the more popular menu selections such as **Save** and **Print**.

(Menu bar and toolbar (reproduced courtesy of Microsoft – www.microsoft.com)

Opening a document

There are several ways to open a document.

❑ *To open a document that you have recently created or modified,* click the **Start** button and select the **My recent documents** option (some versions of Windows may not include this option). This will list the last 15 documents that have been opened.

❑ *To open an existing document from the desktop,* click the **Start** button and select the **My documents** option.

❑ *To open an existing document from within an application,* open the application and access the **File** menu (or click on the **Open** icon on the toolbar). If the document has been opened recently, it may be listed at the bottom of this menu; if not, select the **Open** option, find and click on the required document.

Switching between document windows

When a document is opened (spreadsheet, text, etc.) it is displayed in its own window. The only restriction to the number of documents that can be open at one time (files open) is the capacity of the PC. However, a PC may start to struggle and slow down if trying to handle too many windows at the same time.

To see a list of all windows currently open, click on the **Window** menu at the top of the screen. The tick against one of the filenames indicates that the file is currently in view. To switch to another file, click on its name in this list. This enables the user to switch between files without having to open and close each one individually.

Creating a new document

To create a new document, open the appropriate application and either click on the **New** icon or access the **File** menu and select the **New** option.

Saving a document

It is important to save regularly whenever creating or modifying data. When you are working on a file the information is held in the computer's internal memory and if the power is turned off, the information will be lost. To save a file either access the **File** menu and select the **Save** option or click on the **Save** icon. If saving a file for the first time, select the appropriate folder and give the file a name.

Files and folders

A computer application is used to create and manipulate information. For example, a word-processing application is used to create and manipulate textual documents and a spreadsheet application is designed to create and manipulate tables of numerical data. Regardless of the type of information created, the resulting data is always stored as a computer file. Files can be stored on the computer's hard disk or they can be saved onto removable storage such as a diskette, CD or DVD. When a file is saved it is given a unique and meaningful filename so that it can easily be identified. The user chooses this filename but the file will automatically be given an extension that identifies the application that was used to create it. For example, files created using MS Word are automatically given the extension .DOC, such as *Agenda June 06.DOC.*

Over time the number of files saved on a disk can become unmanageable. This is where folders can prove extremely useful. By creating a number of folders, the user can save their files into the most appropriate folder. For example, a teacher may have a folder for class-work, another for homework and a further folder dedicated to school admin. By saving files into folders it is easier to locate a specific file and open it in order to carry out further modifications.

Printing a document

To print the entire current document, simply click on the **Print** icon. If you want to print just part of the document or multiple copies, access the **File** menu, select the **Print** option and choose the appropriate options from the dialog box.

Closing a document

To close a document either click on the **Close** button at the top right-hand corner of the window or access the **File** menu and select the **Close** option.

Closing an application

To close an application either click on the **Close** button at the top right-hand corner of the application window or access the **File** menu and select the **Exit** option.

Working with applications

⇨ Display the Windows desktop.

⇨ Double-click on an icon to open a word-processing application (MS Word or similar), or click on the **Start** menu and select the **All programs** option to open the application.

⇨ Open a document and print a copy of the first page (using the **File** menu).

⇨ Create a new document and type a few sentences. Print the text by clicking on the **Print** icon. Save the document.

⇨ Close the documents and close the application.

The Internet

This Chapter Considers the resource known as the Internet. If this is a new concept, it is advisable to turn back to Chapter 1 and read the Internet section before continuing. This gives a brief history and overview of the Internet and the World Wide Web and will provide the background necessary to discover more about this amazing learning resource.

The Internet is covered as the first application for two reasons. Firstly it provides a host of information and learning resources that make the life of a teacher that much easier and, secondly, the Internet is such fun to use. This chapter also introduces e-mail, one of the most popular uses of the Internet with literally billions of messages being sent every day. It is hoped that those still harbouring some reticence when it comes to using ICT in a personal setting will find that the Internet and the use of e-mail have distinct advantages and will be encouraged to use them on a regular basis.

Internet Explorer

Internet Explorer is a browser program used to view the web pages that make up the World Wide Web. There are literally billions of web pages available and Explorer provides the facilities to successfully navigate these pages. The easiest way to load Explorer is to double-click on the shortcut icon on the desktop.

If this is not available, click on the **Start** button, select **All programs** and choose **Internet Explorer** from the list.

The toolbar is the main navigational aid to Internet Explorer (the toolbar may look slightly different depending on the version of Explorer being used). Hover over the buttons to find out their functions.

Internet Explorer toolbar (reproduced courtesy of Micosoft – www.microsoft.com)

Viewing a website

Every website has its own unique address known as a Uniform Resource Locator (URL). To access a website simply type the address into the **Address** bar (just below the toolbar) and click on the green **Go** button. For example, the web address for the BBC is www.bbc.co.uk.

Searching for a specific website

In many cases the website address isn't known or the user is searching for specific information rather than a website. This is where a search engine comes in. There are numerous search engines available; some only search registered sites whereas others search the whole Web. Internet Explorer uses the Microsoft search engine MSN as its default search engine. To use this simply click on the **Search** button on the toolbar. Type the keyword(s) such as BBC into the search box and click on the **Search** button. The search engine will provide a list of possible sites.

Other popular search engines are Google, which accounts for 4 out of every 5 searches of the Internet, and Yahoo. To access either of these search engines type the web address into the **Address** bar in the same way as any other website.

Favourites and History

Although there are millions of websites to choose from most Internet users have a few favourites that they return to on a regular basis. To add a site to your favourites, display the website and then access the **Favorites** menu and select the **Add to favorites** option. Change the name of the link if required and click **OK**. To display your favourite sites click on the **Favorites** button on the toolbar. Alternatively you can click on the **History** button to see a list of sites that you have recently visited.

ACTIVITY
Accessing a website

⇨ Load Internet Explorer and hover over the buttons on the toolbar to identify their uses.

⇨ The web address in the **Address** bar will be that of your home page. Delete this entry and type www.bbc.co.uk and click on the **Go** button, to the right of the **Address** bar. The BBC website should load.

⇨ Delete the entry in the **Address** bar and type the web address for your school. Click the **Go** button.

⇨ Click the **Back** button on the toolbar to go back to the BBC site. Click the **Forward** button to access your school website.

⇨ Click on the **Search** button on the toolbar. The MSN search window will appear.

⇨ Type the name of your LEA into the search box. The search window should list some possible sites, with the main window displaying the home pages of these sites. Click on the most appropriate site.

⇨ Click on the **History** button on the toolbar to view a list of sites that you have accessed. Click on the **Favorites** button on the toolbar to see any sites that have been set up as favourites.

⇨ Add your LEA site to your favourites.

⇨ Go back, in turn, to display your school website and the BBC site. Add them to your favourites.

⇨ Type www.google.co.uk into the **Address** bar. Use this search engine to access the site for the QCA (simply type QCA in the search box). Use the Yahoo search engine (www.yahoo.com) to find the site for the DfES. If you are likely to access the QCA or DfES sites regularly, add them to your favourites.

⇨ If you prefer using Google or Yahoo to MSN, add them to your favourites.

⇨ Access the **Tools** menu and select the **Internet options** option. This is where you can change your Internet home page (the site that is automatically loaded each time you open Explorer). This could be your school site, your favourite search engine or any other site that you frequently use. Type the web address of the site in the **Address** box within the **Home page** section. Click **OK**.

⇨ Close Explorer and then open it again to make sure your home page is displayed.

Searching for information

As well as accessing known websites a search engine can also be used to find a whole range of web pages that contain specific information. When searching for information it is likely that the search engine will return a great many 'hits' (pages that contain the specified information). There are a number of steps that can be taken to fine-tune the search.

❑ Be more specific with your search keywords, for example *science* will return millions of hits whereas *key stage 1 science hot and cold* will narrow the field slightly.

❑ Narrowing the search to just UK sites (this option is available with some search engines) will also reduce the hits, but be careful that you are not excluding some useful international information.

❑ Using + before a word specifies that it must appear in the result whereas a – indicates that it should not.

❑ Quotation marks (") around a set of words indicate that the result must contain all the words in the order specified. Without the quotes the result will return any web pages that contain one or more of the words in any order.

❑ An asterisk (*) acts as a wildcard allowing partial matching. This is useful when unsure of spelling, the tense of a word or whether plural.

❑ The AND operator ensures that the search engine will only return web pages containing all the specified words and phrases, for example Viking AND Saxon AND Society.

❑ The OR operator will return those web pages containing any of the specified words or phrases, for example Viking OR Saxon AND Society.

 Not all search engines support AND and OR but most support + and −. Some search engines have an advanced search option that can provide more complex searches.

Surfing the Net

A major attraction of the Internet is the ability to move easily and quickly from one page of information to another. Most web pages include words that are underlined and sometimes displayed in a different colour to the rest of the text (often blue). Hovering the mouse over these highlighted words causes the mouse pointer to change to a hand. The hand-shaped pointer indicates a hyperlink, an address of another web page embedded in the current page. Clicking on the hyperlink opens the new page and clicking on the **Back** button on the toolbar returns to the original page. Links (sometimes known as hot links) are not always displayed as words, sometimes links are embedded within pictures, a button or an icon. Regardless of location, the hand symbol indicates that the link is present.

 When surfing the Net you can end up in some dubious sites. Remember that the information on the World Wide Web has not been verified. Unless you are confident of the credentials of the site always check your information with another site or an alternative source.

Surfing at home

Practice makes perfect. Surfing the Net takes practice and the more you do the better you'll become. Make the time to use the Internet for personal tasks. To get you started try some of the tasks below.

ACTIVITY

Task 1 – the BBC

Access the BBC site at www.bbc.co.uk. Click on the **Change location** box in the **Where I live** area of the page (mid-screen). Type in your postcode and click the **Update** button. The page will now show you local weather. Click on the hyperlink to your local radio and news section. Spend some time exploring the BBC site, getting used to using hyperlinks to move around.

Task 2 – your locality

Access the Up My Street site at www.upmystreet.co.uk. Type in your postcode to display a map of the locality. Use the search box to find a local restaurant. Narrow the search if you have too much choice. Find your most local school (remember, the **Back** button on the toolbar will always take you back to the previous page). Can you find the policing and crime figures for your area? Can you find a link to your local BBC news? If you click on one of the local stories, a new window will open displaying the BBC website. Close the BBC window by clicking on the **Close** button (top right). Explore the Up My Street site some more.

Task 3 – supermarket shopping

If you hate doing the weekly supermarket shopping, have a go at shopping online. All the major supermarkets offer this service and are relatively easy to use. Put aside a couple of hours for the first attempt but after that it won't take as long, as your previous shop will be remembered. It's then just a case of adding to and deleting from this 'template' shop. Use a search engine to find the website of your chosen supermarket and have a go. You will need to have your credit or debit card at the ready.

Task 4 – price comparison

Buying books, CDs and DVDs online is big business with Amazon probably taking the bulk of the online business. Take a look at their site at www.amazon.co.uk. Select the Books tab at the top of the page and type Pride and Prejudice in the Search box. Click the **Go** button. Locate the Oxford World's Classics edition and note the price. Click on the book title to find out more about this edition. Click on **More information** to find out the ISBN (it should read 0192802380).

Amazon is not always the cheapest site. The Internet provides a number of sites that are called price comparison sites such as www.priceguide.co.uk and www.dealtime.co.uk. Access the Price Guide UK site and select **Books** from the displayed options. Type the ISBN for *Pride and Prejudice* (0192802380) into the appropriate box and click the **Search** button. It should display a range of retailers and prices. At the time of writing, several of these options were cheaper than the price of a new copy (rather than second-hand) quoted on Amazon.

Surfing at school

Open Internet Explorer and load your preferred search engine. Complete some or all of the Tasks depending on your confidence and experience of searching the Internet. Once you have found a site that meets your needs, use any hyperlinks to surf the Net to see if you can find further sites providing similar (or more appropriate) information.

ACTIVITY

Task 1 (with help)

You are teaching your class about the Romans and you want to take them on a school trip to find out more about how the Romans lived. Open the Google search engine. Type *Romans school trips* into the search box. How many hits did you get? (should be around 123,000 for UK sites only). Try tightening up your search by specifying the town, *Romans school trips Gloucester*. Not all the sites are specifically about school visits and Google still returns over 45,000 hits. Tighten it up more with *Romans AND school AND visits AND Gloucester*; still over 30,000 hits to wade through. Have one last try, this time insisting that the words school and visit are adjacent, *Romans AND "school visits" AND Gloucester*. Google provides around 250 suggestions.

Repeat this search for your area of the country. Select a suitable site and explore any links to other recommended sites.

Task 2

You want to integrate ICT into a music lesson but need to find out what resources are available. Put together a half-hour lesson plan based on the ideas you find by searching on the keywords *resources ICT music primary*.

Task 3

The head teacher has asked you to provide a five-minute briefing at the next staff meeting on the future developments regarding the teaching of modern languages within primary schools. Search on the keywords *language teaching primary* and find a site that provides the information you need to prepare the talk.

Task 4

You have heard the term Extended Schools but want to know more. Use the Internet to find out what it is all about.

Task 5

See if you can find the latest Ofsted report for your school (tip – if your school has a common name, include the town or village within the keywords).

Task 6

Find out about the use of interactive whiteboards within primary schools. Can you find an organisation in your area that either provides training or demonstration sessions on their use within the classroom?

The Internet in the classroom

Children quickly adapt to the Internet; many will have used it at home to play games and find information. Once you have used the Internet for a while it will become second nature to incorporate its use into classroom sessions, especially for research and confirming information. The most important aspect from a teaching perspective is to ensure that the children appreciate that the information they find cannot necessarily be relied on. They need to appreciate the nature of the Internet and learn to assess information and check validity.

E-mail

E-mail is an abbreviation for 'electronic mail' and is a method of sending messages, electronically, from one computer to another via the Internet. It is a popular and informal method of communication; messages can be sent at any time and they will be received the next time the recipient goes online. E-mail is also a convenient and quick way to send information anywhere in the world; documents, digital photos, pictures, videos and voice recordings can easily be attached to an e-mail.

To use e-mail, a user needs to have an e-mail address. They also need to know the e-mail address of the person they are sending the e-mail to. E-mail addresses are unique and are often provided by an ISP. An e-mail address will usually contain all or part of the user's name followed by an @ symbol, the name of the computer or the Internet server that will store the e-mails and an extension that indicates the type of mail server being used. JoeBloggs@freeserve.com is an example of a typical e-mail address.

E-mail can be accessed from a defined computer using an e-mail program that directs mail to and from the ISP. The two main web browsers Internet Explorer and Netscape Navigator have their associated e-mail programs, Outlook Express and Messenger. There are also many other e-mail programs that can be used if preferred. Alternatively, a web-based e-mail account can be used to send and receive e-mail from any computer with Internet access, providing more flexibility for those who need to pick up e-mails from a number of different computers, anywhere in the world. This is often made available through the ISP or can be accessed free of charge through sites such as Hotmail, Yahoo and Lycos.

ACTIVITY

The following are the generic steps to send an e-mail. The steps have been written with Microsoft Outlook or Outlook Express in mind; however, similar options are available with most mail programs.

⇨ Open your e-mail program and look for a **Mail** button (or similar).

⇨ Look for a **New** (mail or message) or **Compose** button.

⇨ Type the e-mail address for the recipient in the **To** box.

⇨ If you want to copy the e-mail to someone other than the main recipient, type their e-mail address(es) in the **CC** box (Carbon Copy).

⇨ Type the subject of the message in the **Subject** box.

⇨ Type your message – it is usual practice to use informal language when writing an e-mail message.

⇨ Click the **Send** button (or similar).

Experiment with sending further e-mails using spell check facilities and attaching documents to the e-mail. Set up an address book for regular contacts.

E-mail in the classroom

Within schools, e-mail can be an effective method of developing links between the school and the parent/carer body as well as communicating with the wider school community and stakeholders.

From a teaching perspective, the use of e-mail is formally introduced by the QCA scheme of work in Year 3. The implementation of an e-mail system for pupils is complex and varied with the main consideration being safety and security. Conventions for e-mail addressing vary but, in general, emphasis is placed on reducing the risk of unsolicited attention being directed towards pupils from people outside of the school. With this in mind it is unusual for e-mail addresses to reference a child's name.

Schools also need to consider how the e-mail system is set up. In many cases children are able to freely send and receive e-mails within the school but external e-mails are routed through the teacher.

The choice of e-mail program will often depend on the ISP adopted by the school and LEA guidelines. In many cases schools opt for an e-mail system that has child-friendly features. RM EasyMail Plus is a typical example of the web-based e-mail system specifically designed for schools. It provides all the standard features of an e-mail system, such as spell checking, personal address books and personal dictionaries as well as a range of safety features suitable for the target audience. It also comes with a selection of front-end templates making it appropriate for younger children (large buttons and colourful screens) as well as staff (a screen that resembles those designed for adults). A range of similar products is available and it pays to try a few before committing a school to a specific product.

Computer viruses

It would be remiss to close a chapter that discusses the Internet and e-mail without a brief overview of the computer virus. A computer virus is a computer program that has been written with the intent of damaging information held on a computer or in extreme cases making the computer unusable.

There are many ways in which a virus can be introduced to a computer or computer network. The most usual methods are through:

- opening an e-mail attachment that contains a hidden virus

- downloading files from the Internet

- copying a file from an infected CD (or similar).

Anti-virus software can be purchased relatively cheaply and loaded onto a computer to detect viruses. The software continuously scans to detect harmful programs. Anti-virus software is continually being updated to include information about new viruses and it is important to download upgrades from the Internet on a regular basis.

TIP

One of the most common methods of introducing a virus to a computer or network of computers is via a file that is attached to an e-mail. To prevent this type of infection it is advisable to never open an attachment unless the sender of the e-mail is known and the attachment expected.

Useful websites

Google	www.google.co.uk
Hotmail	www.hotmail.com
Lycos	www.lycos.co.uk
RM EasyMail Plus	www.rm.com/easymailplus
Yahoo	www.yahoo.com

CHAPTER 5

ICT and text

This chapter looks at the many ways in which ICT can add value to tasks that involve working with text. Textual documents have just one purpose, to convey information. The information they express can be factual or fictional but the aim is the same, to grab attention and maintain interest.

This chapter concentrates on word-processing and presentation software that has a relevance to primary education and the professional needs of those working within a primary school environment.

Word processing

A word-processing application can be used at many levels, from the glorified typewriter to a publishing tool with the capability to produce multi-chapter documents with table of contents, index, footnotes and multiple styles. The market leader is most certainly Microsoft Word, a functional word-processing package that is ideal for both simple and complex documents. Word is the choice for most businesses and the majority of education authorities have adopted it for the production of administrative documents. Although Word may not be the word processor of choice for the classroom, teachers and support staff need to be familiar with its basic functions for the production of professional documents; a letter produced using a 'child friendly' word processor may be acceptable when printed and posted but if it is e-mailed, the recipient may be less than impressed by the choice of software, particularly if they cannot open the file to read it.

ACTIVITY

Knowing the basics of MS Word is a must. Invest in a good step-by-step guide and spend time getting to grips with the functions that allow you to carry out the following tasks.

⇨ Create, open, save, print and close a document.

⇨ Create a letter, spell check, save and print it.

⇨ Produce a document with bold headings, italic text and bulleted lists.

⇨ Proof-read and spell check your document and use the editing features to make changes and improve the document.

⇨ Change the format of the text (font, size, colour of text). Add page numbers.

⇨ Use the thesaurus to improve the content.

⇨ Create a document that can be used for your school website. Insert photos and scanned work into the document.

⇨ Create a document that contains a table.

These skills will provide the expertise you need to confidently communicate with school stakeholders and the wider community. They will also provide the knowledge and understanding to pick up and run with any of the word-processing applications designed specifically for the primary market.

Word processing in the classroom

Although MS Word can provide most of the functionality to cover the required text-handling aspects of the ICT schemes of work it does not have a word or picture bank facility. It can also be difficult to navigate for the younger child. For these reasons, the majority of schools tend to use specialist word-processing software for Foundation and Key Stage 1 with some schools introducing Word in the latter stages of Key Stage 2 in preparation for high school.

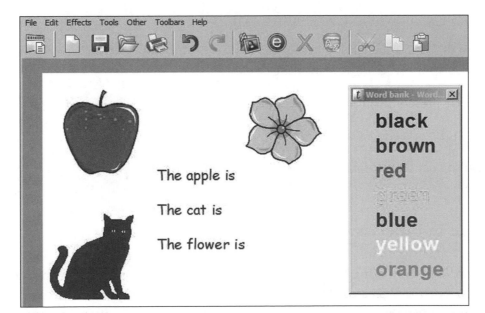

Textease Studio CT, a word bank (screenshots used with permission of Softease – www. softease.com)

Word and picture banks are used in Foundation and Key Stage 1 to introduce the children to using a computer to structure a simple sentence. The teacher can either use a predefined bank of words that comes as part of the package or they can create their own (a picture bank is a bank of pictures rather than words). The children can then drag and drop the appropriate word (or picture) into the spaces to compose a sentence.

Presentation software

Microsoft PowerPoint is the usual tool of choice when producing a slide-show type presentation for colleagues, parents or other school stakeholders. The pre-prepared PowerPoint presentation can be displayed on an electronic whiteboard or screen and although simplicity is often the key, PowerPoint does also provide a host of visual and sound effects for the more adventurous. Presentation software is designed to use multimedia, combining text, data, pictures, video, web pages and sound to convey information. Accordingly it could feature in several of the chapters in this section.

For your own professional development it is worth getting to grips with MS PowerPoint. Not only will it help you teach the children about presenting using multimedia it will also stand you in good stead when mentoring staff, cascade training colleagues, presenting to stake-holders or attending interviews. Again, find a book that provides easy to follow step-by-step instructions and use it to complete the following tasks.

1) Create a new blank presentation, select a slide layout and create a simple text slide.

2) Learn how to insert new slides, delete slides and re-order slides.

3) Change slide information, text formats and create notes for your slides.

4) Use the drawing toolbar, backgrounds, colours, AutoShapes and Clipart to make your presentation more visually appealing.

5) Print your presentation.

6) Create and run a slide show.

7) Use timings and annotations, hidden slides and animation effects.

Presentation in the classroom

Older children will enjoy using PowerPoint however for the earlier years it may be more practical to use software such as 2Create a Story, a multimedia package designed to incorporate pictures, sound and text. Integrated packages similar to Textease Studio CT often include presentation modules that provide facilities to create slides and run a slide show. It is worth noting that in some cases these tend to be of a similar complexity to MS PowerPoint and there are few benefits in using the 'child friendly' product.

Useful websites

2Create a Story	www.2simple.com
PowerPoint	www.microsoft.com
Textease Studio CT	www.softease.com
Word	www.microsoft.com

CHAPTER 6

ICT and data

This chapter looks at the ways in which ICT can add value to the presentation and manipulation of data. In the primary setting this involves the use of spreadsheet, database and datalogging software with their associated graphing features.

Databases

A database is simply information that is stored in a defined way; the data is stored as individual records with each record comprising a defined range of fields. The telephone directory is the most common example of a database; the directory is the database with each entry in the directory being a record and each item within that record being a field (name, address, telephone number are all fields). Another example of a manual database is a card box or filing system, much like those used by school receptionists before the days of computerised records. Each card or file holds information on an individual child; the card box or filing cabinet is the database and each card or file a record. Each record contains the same fields; pupil number, name, gender, date of birth, age, contact details, start date, etc. The data is usually sorted alphabetically or numerically so that an individual record can easily be found; for example, a telephone directory is ordered by surname and school records can be stored in order of name or pupil number.

Computer databases work in the same way except there is much more flexibility in the way that data can be viewed. The data can be sorted based on any of the fields so, for example, the school data could be viewed with respect to date of birth so it is easy to identify children with a birthday on any particular day. Speed is another issue; computerised databases are much quicker to search. Finding the school record card for a specific child may take a minute or two using a bank of filing cabinets whereas the computerised data can be accessed in seconds.

The fields that make up a database can be of several types:

Database fields

Text	Character data such as name, address, next of kin
Number	Numeric data such as age, height, weight
Date	Date type data such as date of birth, start date (at school)
Logical	Logical data such as yes/no, true/false, female/male
Comment	A comment is free text that adds value to the record; the database cannot be searched on a comment field
Picture	Some databases allow a picture field to illustrate the record – this is common with database products designed for children or databases requiring a photograph for identification; data cannot be sorted on a picture field.

ACTIVITY

On a professional basis teachers and support staff will not have much call to use complex database software. There may be need to access pupil records but if this is the case, training should be provided. However, in order to teach database principles, it is important to understand how a computerised database is designed, how data is added and how the database is queried (individual records searched for).

To do this:

⇨ Ask the staff in your school office to demonstrate the database system they use to store pupil information.

⇨ Spend some time experimenting with database software designed for primary education. Create a simple database, add some records, sort the database and search for specific information.

⇨ Database software usually provides options to display data in various graphical formats from pictograms to bar and pie charts. Have a look at the options available and compare products.

Databases in the classroom

Databases are formally introduced in Year 3 with branching databases being introduced in Year 4 (although the concepts are discussed in Year 2). The Microsoft database product Access is complex and not suitable for primary aged children. Alternative software is abundant, some forming components of integrated packages and others serving as specialised products. Many of the products available include example databases that are already populated with data and can be used for the various activities suggested within the QCA schemes of work. For example, several include a database of mini-beasts that can be linked to science topics. The vast majority of products also allow the teacher to create and populate their own databases so that the ICT skill can be learnt within a current curriculum topic.

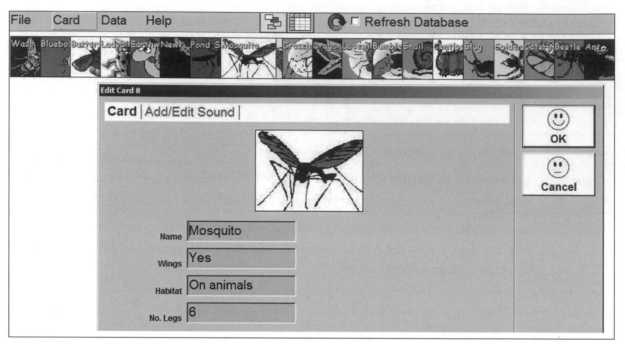

Database record for the mosquito, 2Investigate (screenshot used with permission from 2Simple – www.2simple.com)

The 2Investigate software is just one example of a database program designed for younger children. It is essentially a content-free tool although some example databases are included to demonstrate the program and provide data for activities. This package also includes a feature to produce a Venn diagram, an unusual yet interesting addition. This is an ideal tool for introducing pupils to databases but may be too simplistic for older children.

Database products designed for primary education usually provide options for providing graphical representations of the data such as pictograms, bar charts, pie charts and line graphs.

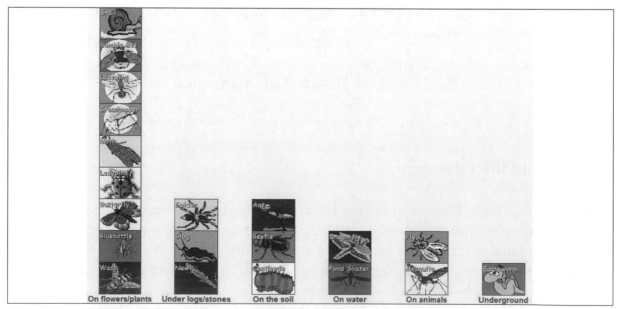

Pictogram showing habitat, 2Investigate (screenshot used with permission from 2Simple – www.2simple.com)

Branching databases   A branching database is sometimes referred to as a binary tree or decision tree. It provides a visual representation of data that can be separated into subgroups based on yes/no decisions.

Several integrated products such as Textease Studio CT provide branching database capability. There are also a number of dedicated branching database programs such as FlexiTREE 2 or BlackCat Software's Decisions3.

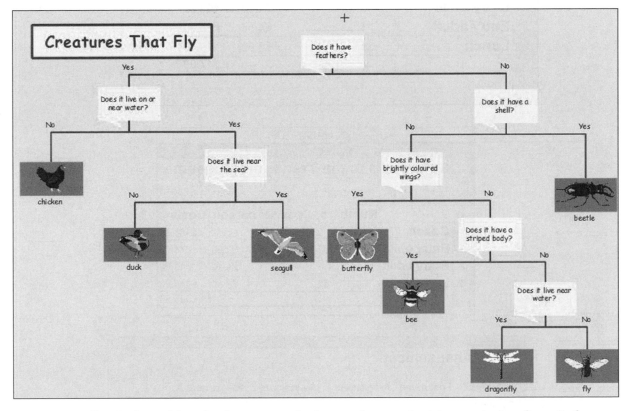

Textease Studio CT branching database example (screenshot used with permission from Softease – www.softease.com)

Spreadsheets

A spreadsheet is generally a table of data with column and row totals. A computerised spreadsheet consists of cells with each cell being defined by a unique cell address. The cell is formed where a row and column intersect. Rows are labelled numerically and columns alphabetically; for example, the cell formed where column C intersects row 6 is known as cell C6. Labels, data and formulae are entered into the cells.

Creating a computerised spreadsheet is not really any different from producing a costing model on the back of an envelope but the beauty is you don't need to work out the totals for yourself. The software does it for you and, more importantly, if you change a value, you will instantly see how that change affects the rest of the data in the sheet. So, for instance, taking the school trip example on page 48, if the number of children increases to 37 the new total will automatically update.

Microsoft Excel - Costing model

File   Edit   View   Insert   Format   Tools   Data   Window   Help

D8 | fx =B8*C8

	A	B	C	D	E
1	**School trip to the Transport Museum**				
2					
3					
4		**Numbers**	**Cost per person**	**Costs**	
5	**Coach**			£150.00	
6	**Entry child**	30	£2.00	£60.00	
7	**Entry adult**	4	£4.50	£18.00	
8	**Lunch**	34	£3.50	£119.00	
9				£347.00	
10					
11					

D9 | fx =SUM(D5:D8)

	A	B	C	D
1	**School trip to the Transport Museum**			
2				
3				
4		**Numbers**	**Cost per person**	**Costs**
5	**Coach**			£150.00
6	**Entry child**	37	£2.00	£74.00
7	**Entry adult**	4	£4.50	£18.00
8	**Lunch**	41	£3.50	£143.50
9				£385.50

	A	B	C	D	E	F
1	**ICT Assessment**					
2						
3	Surname	First name	Assessment 1	Assessment 2	Assessment 3	
4	Brown	Joe	67	72	70	
5	Green	Sarah	43	38	50	
6	Smith	Jane	80	89	92	
7	Ali	Osman	65	72	75	
8	Hali	Jess	54	58	71	
9						

Microsoft Excel (screenshots courtesy of Microsoft – www.microsoft.com)

The majority of spreadsheet programs also include graphing features to provide a more visual representation of the data.

As a teacher or support assistant you will find spreadsheet software invaluable for assessment and record keeping. Microsoft Excel is a popular spreadsheet package that is generally accepted as the market leader in the business world. Education authorities tend to use Excel to produce budgets and financial projections and this has filtered down to internal school financial planning and assessment. It is advisable to invest in a step-by-step guide to Excel and familiarise yourself with the following tasks:

⇨ Create a simple spreadsheet containing labels (title, row and column headings) and data. Save the spreadsheet.

⇨ Create simple formulae to total the rows and columns, C3+C4+C5. Save and print.

⇨ Change some data and observe the resulting change to the totals.

⇨ Progress to using the SUM function to total adjacent cells.

⇨ Learn how to copy, paste and move the contents of cells.

You may choose to increase your spreadsheet skills further but these tasks will give you the knowledge and expertise to use spreadsheets within classroom activities and produce management reports, assessments and forecasts. You will also find that these skills are transferable to the spreadsheet packages designed specifically for children.

Spreadsheets in the classroom

Spreadsheets are introduced in Year 5 with further features being introduced in Year 6. In both years there are ample opportunities to teach the ICT skill while documenting the results from science experiments.

Spreadsheet packages designed specifically for children have the look and feel of MS Excel with simplified functionality. Textease CT, for example, has a spreadsheet module which allows the child to create a spreadsheet template of the required size within the standard Textease window. The functionality is the same as Excel with formula being created using a Formula box.

As with all software try out a few and ask for recommendations from colleagues at other schools before purchasing.

Textease Studio CT spreadsheet feature (screenshot used with permission from Softease – www. softease.com)

Datalogging

Introduced in Year 5, computerised datalogging is a method of monitoring and measuring environmental conditions such as changes in temperature, noise or movement. This activity requires both hardware and software; the hardware is the datalogging device that is used to collect the data and the software the computer program that reads and presents that data. The datalogger can either be attached to the computer when logging the data or used remotely and then

The LogIT Explorer datalogger from DCP Microdevelopments and the Log Box from TTS

attached to the computer at a later time to download the data. The datalogger will either come with built-in sensors or with a selection of sensors that can be attached depending on the task.

There are a number of software products designed specifically for the primary school market. Some suppliers provide both the software and the datalogging hardware whereas others provide just one or the other. For example, Data Harvest provides EasySense Q3, a product that includes both the hardware and the software, although each component can be purchased separately. Logotron, however, only produces the software, Junior Datalogging Insight, but works closely with other suppliers to make sure that it is fully compatible with their datalogging hardware.

There are new products available all the time; the Log Box from TTS is a prototype at the time of writing but promises to be an affordable option from late 2006; it comes with a range of sensors and software for capturing, storing, graphing and analysing results. It is always advisable to spend some time looking at a few products before purchasing.

Useful websites

2Investigate	www.2simple.com
BlackCat Decisions3	www.blackcatsoftware.com/products/decisions3. asp
EasySense Q3	www. data-harvest.co.uk/datalogging/esq3-g.html
FlexiTREE 2	www.flexible.co.uk/FlexiTREE.html
Junior Datalogging Insight	www.logo.com/cat/view/junior-datalogging.html
Log Box (TTS)	www.log-box.co.uk
LogIT Explorer	www.dcpmicro.com/logit/explorer/index.htm
Microsoft Excel	www.microsoft.com
Textease Studio CT	www.softease.com

CHAPTER 7

ICT and creativity

This chapter considers the important part that ICT can play when developing the creative skills of children. The opportunities are endless; however, it is important that the exposure to computer packages is not to the detriment of the more traditional methods of producing artistic and creative representations.

Computer graphics

Both manual and computerised methods of producing art or technical drawings have distinct advantages and disadvantages and it is vital that children are shown how to use ICT for creative tasks but are also encouraged to consider the limitations that computer graphics packages can have.

The purpose of a computer graphic is just the same as a manually produced illustration: the aim is to provide a visual representation either to enhance or replace textual information. A computer graphic can be a drawing, a painting, a scanned image, a photograph, a diagram, model or a combination of any of these pictorial forms. Once created a computer graphic can be saved and used within a whole range of documentation; it can be changed, enhanced and generally manipulated to suit the purpose.

Computer images can be divided into three types – bitmap, vector and metafile – with each type having distinct advantages and disadvantages depending on the use and the type of image being created. A graphic file can usually be recognised by the file type (identified by the three-letter extension following the filename). This will either identify the type of graphic file or the computer package that was used to create it.

Bitmap graphics

Computer graphics packages that store images in bitmap format are generally used for creating paintings. Microsoft Paint is a popular example of this type of package. Images are created as a series of tiny dots or pixels where each pixel can be manipulated providing a high degree of flexibility and accuracy, making it ideal for producing paintings. Once created the picture can be edited by zooming in on the image so that the individual pixels can be added, removed or the colour changed.

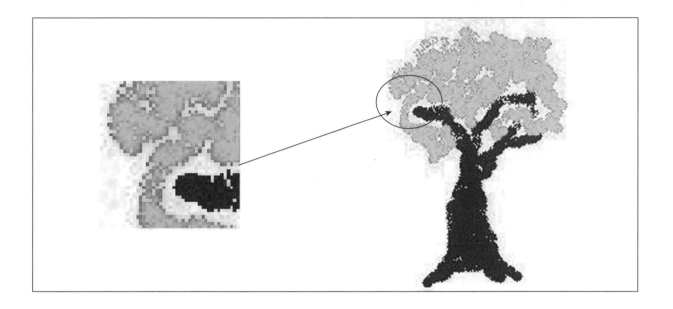

An image created in this way has a single dimension; if an area of the picture is painted over, the original image is removed. For example, if a background is painted and then a figure is added 'on top' of the background, the figure will replace the background. If the figure is subsequently erased, the picture will contain a 'hole'; the background will not reappear behind the figure. This can prove a disadvantage if creating an image that requires the layering and moving of objects such as creating a collage or diagram. This type of image is also at a disadvantage when it comes to rescaling. If the image is enlarged, the edge of the picture becomes distorted and jagged and the individual pixels become more apparent, reducing the quality of the picture.

Bitmap files are often saved as BMP or PCX file types; both are large and can be slow to download if sending an image via the Internet. It is usual practice to save a BMP or PCX file as JPEG format (with JPG extension) especially if transporting the file or storing a large number of images. The JPG file is a compressed version of the original; this does reduce the number of colours in the image but the file will be a much more manageable size. Many bitmap graphics programs have this option but if not, the graphic can be opened in a package such as Paint Shop Pro and saved in the compressed format.

Digital photographs are saved as bitmap graphics (usually as JPEGs). The photo is made up of thousands of dots or bits; the greater the bpi (bits per inch) the better the quality of the photo.

ACTIVITY

Microsoft Paint is not the easiest package to use but if you master the basics, the paint packages aimed at the primary market will be straightforward.

⇨ Open MS Paint (it can be found under Accessories). The drawing and painting tools are displayed at the left-hand side of the screen.

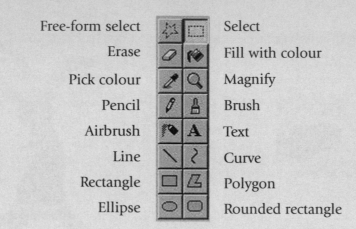

Free-form select			Select
Erase			Fill with colour
Pick colour			Magnify
Pencil			Brush
Airbrush			Text
Line			Curve
Rectangle			Polygon
Ellipse			Rounded rectangle

⇨ Experiment with the different tools. You may find that the **Undo** option from the **Edit** menu is easier than using the **Erase** tool if you make an error.

⇨ Paint a picture of the sky, grass and trees. Use the **Magnify** tool to see the individual pixels that make up the picture. Change the colour of an individual pixel. Zoom back out. Select one of the trees in your picture and cut and paste it to a different position. Fill in the resulting gap with appropriate background.

Vector graphics

Vector-based graphics packages, often referred to as object-based graphics packages, store images as mathematical coordinates. An image comprises a number of objects with each object being identified by its coordinates within the image as a whole; much like drawing a shape on squared paper and noting the coordinates on the matrix. As an example, a curve is saved as the data that represents the points through which the curve passes and a rectangle as the coordinates of the outline of the shape. Information is also held on the thickness of the lines and colour. This method of saving the image means that objects can be rescaled without losing resolution and an object can be layered, copied, resized, rotated and moved without affecting any other object that makes up the image. This type of graphics package is ideal for graphical modelling, CAD applications (Computer Aided Design), collage work and producing diagrams.

ACTIVITY

The drawing tools in MS Word and PowerPoint are adequate for most requirements and are certainly suitable for gaining experience in creating vector graphics. If you find you have more complex tasks, specialist commercial software such as CorelDRAW, Macromedia Flash and Adobe Illustrator will provide more sophisticated features.

⇨ Open MS Word and create a new document. Display the Draw toolbar if not already displayed (access the **View** menu and select **Toolbars**).

Microsoft Word Draw toolbar (reproduced courtesy of Microsoft – www.microsoft.com)

⇨ Move the cursor across each tool in turn to see what it does. Experiment with the tools.

⇨ Draw a rectangle and fill it with green. Draw a circle or ellipse to overlap the rectangle and fill it with black. Select **AutoShapes** and select a shape from the **Stars and banners** shapes. Place it on top of the circle and colour it with a pale colour.

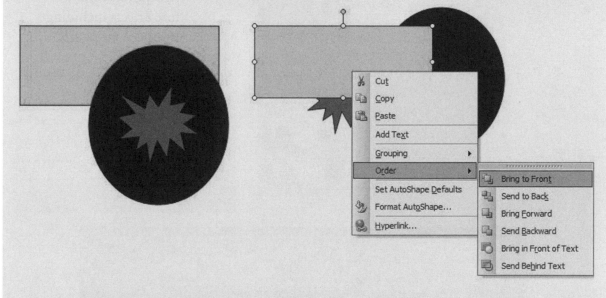

Microsoft Word drawing features (reproduced by courtesy of Microsoft – www.microsoft.com)

⇨ Move the objects around and change the order by right-clicking on the object and selecting the **Order** option.

Metafile graphics

The third type of graphic is a combination of the first two: it is an object created using vector graphics yet filled with a bitmap pattern. Clipart images are often supplied as metafiles; they can be resized and yet still maintain resolution. Metafile graphics are ideal when requiring an illustration to fill a defined space. The graphic can be resized and stretched to fit. The most common metafile formats are WMF (Windows Metafile), EMF (Enhanced Metafile) and CGM (Computer Graphics Metafile).

Graphics in the classroom

There are a host of graphics programs designed specifically for children. Some stand alone but many form part of an integrated software package including many, if not all, of the features required to teach ICT at primary level. Textease CT is a good example of an integrated package that includes both a paint program (producing bitmap images) and a graphics program (producing vector images).

The Textease Studio CT paint palette (shown) includes similar features to MS Paint but also incorporates some 'fun' effects including multi-colour paints.

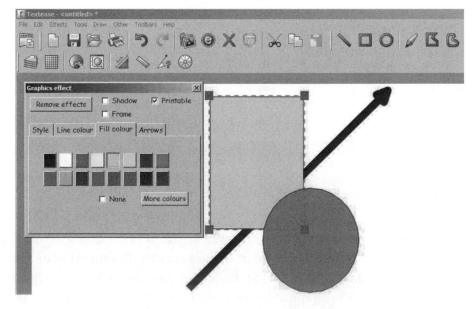

Textease Studio CT graphics features (screenshots used with permission of Softease – www. softease.com)

The graphics tools (opposite) provide similar features to MS Word.

Computer graphics can be introduced as early as the Foundation Stage and are integrated into activities across the curriculum throughout Key Stages 1 and 2. For example, for younger children, computer graphics can form part of the development of story writing.

The 2Create a Story program integrates a paint program with text creation. The screen is divided into two, allowing the children to type their story in the lower half of the screen while illustrating the text above.

This program also allows the children to add sounds to the story, providing a comprehensive multimedia tool.

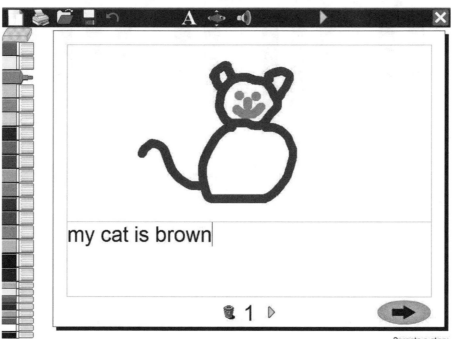

2Create a Story (screenshot used with permission from 2Simple – www.2simple.com)

Older children, particularly when looking at graphical modelling in Year 5, can benefit from computer graphics programs designed specifically for the task such as FlexiCAD, a drafting program designed for primary and secondary education.

These are just a few of the innovative examples of computer programs that integrate graphics. There are many more on the market and it is always worth asking friends and colleagues for personal recommendations.

ICT and music

There are a number of computer packages available that are designed for composing music, from those designed for the primary curriculum through to commercial packages designed for the home market. The latter tend to be aimed at older children (Key Stage2) and simulate a recording studio, providing features to create and mix music.

The 2Simple Music Toolkit is just one example of software specifically designed to meet the curriculum requirements. It comprises a number of modules including a facility to compose and record music. Again, recommendation is the best route if looking for suitable software.

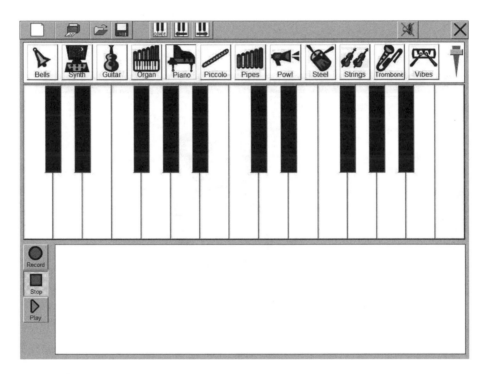

2Simple Music Toolkit (screenshots used with permission from 2Simple – www.2simple.com)

Useful websites

2Create a Story	www.2simple.com
2Simple Music Toolkit	www.2simple.com
Abobe Illustrator	www.adobe.com/uk
CorelDRAW	www.corel.co.uk
FlexiCAD	www.flexible.co.uk
Macromedia Flash	www.adobe.com/uk
Microsoft Paint	www.microsoft.com
Paint Shop Pro	www.corel.co.uk
Textease Studio CT	www.softease.com

CHAPTER 8

ICT and control

> The control element of the ICT curriculum is often the area that causes the most difficulty for teachers. This chapter is designed to look at the basic concepts of control by providing an introduction to the technology as well as the possible applications.

The control technology units within the QCA ICT schemes of work are designed specifically to introduce children to simple programming instructions and to develop logical thought. During the Foundation Stage and Year 1, practical activities are used to establish the significance of instructions and the importance of following commands in sequence. Children are also introduced to machines with the emphasis on basic control. In Year 2 children learn how to program floor robots, progressing in Year 4 to controlling screen robots using a 'Logo' type language. In Years 5 and 6 children develop their programming skills by instructing the computer to control electrical devices such as bulbs, buzzers, light sensors and pressure pads.

The QCA schemes of work (see the Standards website) provide a comprehensive set of activities for all stages of control technology development. These suggested activities require investment in specialist software and equipment as well as full class participation. Budgets are always tight within schools; however, it is important to ensure that the children have access to equipment and are not passive observers of a teacher demonstration.

Controlling a floor or screen robot

Floor robots

The floor robot is a programmable, battery-driven 'toy' that moves around the floor based on the given instructions. At a cost of £100 or more, coupled with the running costs of replacement batteries, floor robots can represent a hefty investment for many nurseries and small primary schools. Recent additions to the market are more affordable, costing around £40 with design features to attract younger children such as a smiling face and large eyes. Controls are usually situated on the back of the robot with four directional keys and Go, Clear and Pause buttons. Sounds or flashing eyes are used to confirm that each instruction has been executed.

The Bee-Bot® (picture provided by TTS Group – www.beebot.co.uk)

The Roamer floor turtle made by Valiant Technology is a popular choice for many primary schools with the Bee-Bot® from TTS providing an affordable option for younger children. The PIPPIN and PIXIE, supplied by Swallow Systems, are other examples of programmable vehicles designed for use in primary schools and nurseries.

ACTIVITY

Information and links to resources can be found on the manufacturers' websites. Alternatively, access the Kent NGfL, Primary Resources or the Sir Robert Hitcham's Primary School websites for a range of activities. Some activities are device specific but they can easily be adapted for other programmable toys.

Screen robots

Programming a screen robot/turtle provides the next developmental stage in logical and instructional sequencing. Introduced formally in Year 4, children learn how to enter instructions to control a screen robot to draw lines and shapes on the computer screen.

Manipulating the screen robot involves writing instructions. The children learn to give single instructions and then progress to produce a sequence of instructions known as a procedure. The programming language used to write the instructions is known as 'Logo'. The Logo language was developed in the 1960s by Seymour Papert and was specifically designed to be suitable for children as well as adults.

Logo programs differ slightly but in general the commands are similar. A basic instruction involves the direction followed by the distance, for example Forward 50 will move the screen robot forward 50 steps (drawing a line as it moves). The robot can then be turned using an instruction such as Right 90, to turn the robot right through 90 degrees. The commands Pendown and Penup (or similar) are used to move the robot with or without drawing.

There are numerous 'Logo' packages that are suitable for use within a primary school. One of the most established products is SuperLogo which until recently was produced by Logotron Educational Software. Although no longer available from new, SuperLogo has been superseded by Imagine Logo

(Primary), a similar program with enhanced functionality. Alternatively, MSWLogo from Softronix, is a simple but effective version of Logo that is downloadable from the Internet (free of charge). The Softronix website also provides teaching resources and links to other sites.

ACTIVITY

The Internet provides a host of examples and activities for teaching the Logo language. As a starting point, access the Primary Resources site for a range of activities and handouts including lists of the Logo commands and example programs.

Controlling devices

The QCA ICT Unit 5E involves using a programming language to control simple devices such as buzzers, small motors and lights via a basic control box. Initially the children learn how to control the devices by turning them on and off and then progress to sequence a set of instructions to achieve a set outcome. For example, an initial activity may involve programming a light to come on for a set time and then turn off again. The children then progress to more complex tasks such as controlling a set of disco lights or traffic lights. The children learn how to produce a simple flowchart of the process and then write a program to carry out the instructions.

For example, a program to switch on a light, wait for 5 seconds, switch the light off again and then switch on a buzzer, wait for 5 seconds and then switch it off again may look like this (where the light bulb is attached to the first output on the control box and the buzzer to the second output):

Switch on output 1
Wait 5
Switch off output 1
Switch on output 2
Wait 5
Switch off output 2

Unit 6C progresses to show the children how to use input devices or switches to control a process. They are shown how to attach devices such as pressure pads, light sensors, magnetic switches and on/off switches to a control box. They then program the computer to carry out a process where a change is detected. For example, the task may involve switching on the light when it gets dark or sounding a buzzer when a pressure pad is pressed. To do this they need to learn the control language required to program the control box to make such decisions (using the commands 'if … then …').

It is preferable to teach Units 5E and 6C using dedicated hardware (control boxes, lights, buzzers, light sensors, pressure sensors, programmable robots, etc.) along with the associated software to program the devices. However, this is not always possible within the school environment, sometimes due to financial implications or, on occasion, through lack of teacher expertise. One solution is to team up with another school and share equipment/expertise or to work with a local High School or City Learning Centre where experts within this field can provide tuition.

On the occasions when the hardware is not available, the control software can be used to simulate the control process. The majority of software products provide an interface to the hardware as well as simulated control. Junior Control Insight from Logotron, CoCo 3 from the Commotion Group and Flowol 3 from Data Harvest are examples of popular products that provide both facilities. The children use the software to write a series of commands either as a program or flowchart. The instructions are then used to control the electrical devices and sensors that are plugged into an external control box or to simulate the effect on the screen.

ACTIVITY

Although simulation is not recommended as a replacement for dedicated hardware, it does provide an excellent way to reinforce the concepts learnt through practical sessions.

The Control Box

Control boxes come in all shapes and sizes. Data Harvest produces the FlowGo control box designed to work with the Flowol 3 software. The FlowGo control box can be operated while plugged into the computer or the program can be downloaded into its memory so that the FlowGo can run the program independently while disconnected from the computer.

FlowGo control box from Data Harvest (www.data-harvest.co.uk)

ACTIVITY

To get an clearer idea as to how this might work, run the online video at www.data-harvest.co.uk/control/flowgo_p_g.html.

As a more fun approach, Commotion produces the CoCo the Clown control box. Shaped like the head of a clown, CoCo has bulbs to illuminate the eyes and a ping-pong ball nose, a buzzer for a mouth and a motor to rotate the bow tie.

Control software simulation

Control software can be used to simulate the results of the programmed instructions through animated graphics displayed on the computer screen. For example, a program to turn a light bulb on and off can be displayed as an animated light bulb on the screen, switching on and off as dictated by the program. Flowol 3 displays the resulting effects using an animated 'mimic'. Mimics are either 3-D or 2-D pictures/photographs including a kitchen scene, a road scene with traffic lights and a fire engine. The aim is for the children to explore control technology within a 'real life' context. Take a look at the suppliers' websites for examples.

Programmable robots and vehicles

There are also several products that use the Duplo, Lego or K'nex ranges of products to create buggies that can be controlled via programming instructions. In fact, product developers are always looking for new and innovative ways to stimulate interest and Commotion has recently risen to the challenge by creating the RoboDance. This provides a fun way for schools to carry out control technology by building a Robodancer using the LEGO Team Challenge Sets that can be purchased from the Commotion website (with a little creativity any LEGO set can be used). The children build a prescribed buggy (LEGO RoboDance Robot) following a simple PowerPoint guide and then program a dance routine for their robot.

Controlling a K'nex model (picture courtesy of Data Harvest – www.data-harvest.co.uk)

Control technology is an area where children really can have fun but it is important to remember that the aim is to teach the importance of planning before programming. Encouraging the children to flow chart the process before programming will stand them in good stead for future challenges. By taking the time to logically work through the task they will produce accurate programming instructions that generate the intended result.

Useful websites

Commotion Group	www.schoolmarket.co.uk
Data Harvest	www.data-harvest.co.uk
Sir Robert Hitcham's Primary School	www.hitchams.suffolk.sch.uk/foundation/pixie/index.htm
Kent NGfL	www.kented.org.uk/NGfL/ict/robots/games.html
Logotron	www.logo.com
Primary Resources	www.primaryresources.co.uk/ict/ict4.htm
Softronics	www.softronix.com/logo.html
Standards Site (DfES)	www.standards.dfes.gov.uk/schemes2/it
Swallow Systems	www.swallow.co.uk
TTS Group	www.beebot.co.uk
Valiant Technology	www.valiant-technology.com

PART C

INTEGRATING ICT INTO THE CURRICULUM

The final section of this book concentrates on the ways in which ICT can successfully be integrated into the curriculum for all stages within primary education. It is divided into three chapters covering the Pre-school and Foundation Stage, Key Stage 1 and Key Stage 2. For each stage within primary education consideration is given to the statutory requirements for teaching ICT as well as the need to successfully apply ICT across the curriculum.

Does ICT add value to a child's education?

It is possibly rather late on in this book to ask this but nevertheless it is a vital question. For some the answer is clear: ICT is a fantastic tool that encourages innovation and benefits learning at every level. Others may feel less enthusiastic but still believe that ICT is here to stay and therefore should be used to its best advantage within education. At the other end of the spectrum there are those who are more cautious, doubting the benefits of ICT and questioning whether it does actually improve standards.

Recent research shows (Becta, 2005) that there are measurable benefits.

Schools judged by OFSTED to have very good ICT resources achieved better results than schools with poor ICT. The difference between the two groups of schools has increased in comparison with the results for the previous year. The very good ICT schools had improved their performance and the poor ICT schools had got worse overall. This difference was also seen for schools in similar socio-economic circumstances. When schools with similar socio-economic backgrounds were compared, those with good ICT resources tended to achieve better results than those with unsatisfactory ICT.

Of course there are many factors that affect performance; ICT is just one aspect. Educationalists remain divided on the benefits of ICT as an educational tool, however. Regardless of personal views, it is a fact that ICT is here to stay and our children are going to grow and develop in a world where technology plays an important part.

Embedding ICT in primary schools

The emphasis on embedding ICT within education is apparent in reports, the media and on the agendas of the major teaching conferences, but is it actually happening? A recent study carried out by Ofsted (Ofsted, 2005) found that although the use of ICT as a learning tool is on the increase, none of the schools taking part in the study embedded ICT to the extent that it was an everyday aspect of pupils' learning.

The report came up with a number of interesting observations, including:

❏ The involvement of senior managers, especially the head teacher, was the most critical factor in good ICT leadership.

❏ Few schools built ICT as a tool for raising standards into their strategic planning.

❏ Most schools made at least satisfactory curriculum provision for ICT, including some balance between teaching ICT capability and its application across subjects.

❏ Most primary schools had a good range of hardware and software, including digital still and video cameras. However, many pupils did not have sufficient access to computers to support their learning across the curriculum on a regular basis.

❏ The Internet was used quite extensively by older primary pupils for research in a range of subjects, while the use of IWBs in schools facilitated cross-curricular links.

❏ It was found that in primary schools, ICT is used mainly to support English and mathematics; there was some use of ICT in other subjects but application across the curriculum is still largely undeveloped.

The aim of this part is to help teachers make ICT an everyday aspect of pupils' learning by providing suggestions of ways in which ICT can be used across the curriculum. It is imperative that teachers move away from the mindset that they need to teach their pupils an ICT skill and instead look for meaningful ways in which that skill can be learned 'on the job'. For example, rather than teaching a class how to create a spreadsheet, the spreadsheet can be used as a means of displaying data from a science experiment.

ICT resources

There are a host of ICT resources available for primary school teachers and support staff. Some resources are free, others come at a price; some are good or even excellent and some are poor. The difficulty comes with sorting the wheat from the chaff. A simple search on the Internet will usually produce pages of matches and it can be a time-consuming exercise finding a product that is suitable.

To make life easier the government has created the Curriculum Online website to provide a comprehensive directory of products that have been assessed for quality and suitability. It has also allocated substantial funds in the form of eLCs (electronic learning credits) that can be used to purchase the resources that are included on the website. This eLC money is given directly to a school to spend on the multimedia resources they require. No transactions take place directly through the Curriculum Online site; once a product has been selected it is ordered direct from a supplier as an eLC purchase.

Free resources

As well as the resources that can be purchased with eLCs there are numerous excellent free resources available on the Internet. Again, quality can vary but by sticking with the well-known names or recommended sites it is easy and quick to build up a portfolio of educational games and simulations that can add interest to a session.

Some of the suggested activities within the following chapters include websites offering appropriate free resources. It is important to note that websites often change and links can be broken. If a link is not working, go to the home page for the site and search for the resource.

Published schemes of work

The majority of the major publishing houses have produced comprehensive learning resources for teaching ICT at primary level. These usually consist of pupil books, teacher guides and supporting CD-ROMs (compact disc read-only memory) that closely follow the QCA schemes of work. The CD-ROMs generally include simulated applications for music, control and database activities, making the overall package completely self-sufficient. Sold directly to schools some can be purchased using eLCs and although somewhat costly they can provide all the resources required to successfully integrate ICT in one convenient package. Although similar in content, the design and approach can differ and it is worth looking at a few before purchasing. HarperCollins ICT Adventure and Nelson Thornes ICT Handbooks/Integrated Tasks/Trouble shooters are two of the more popular schemes.

📖 Useful references and websites

Becta, 2005 – *Becta Report: Primary Schools – ICT and Standards*: www.becta.org.uk/research/research.cfm?section1id230

Ofsted, 2005 – *Embedding ICT in schools – a dual evaluation exercise*, December 2005: www.ofsted.gov.uk/publications/index.cfm?fuseactionpubs.summary&id4128

Curriculum Online	www.curriculumonline.gov.uk
HarperCollins ICT Adventure (Elston and Orrell, 2001–06)	www.collinseducation.com
Nelson Thornes ICT Handbooks/Integrated Tasks/Troubleshooters	www.nelsonthornes.com

Further useful sites are listed in Appendix B.

CHAPTER 9

Pre-school and Foundation Stage

This chapter is designed for those teaching children within the Foundation Stage of primary education (nursery and reception), arguably the most important period for exposure to ICT with children quickly adapting to mouse control and the operation of simple computer games and activities.

The issue of when to introduce ICT to children has prompted some disagreement among teachers. While the importance of exposure to ICT during the Foundation Stage is a view shared by many, some practitioners have questioned the introduction of computer technologies to formal education at such an early age. This is an area for continued discussion although, undoubtedly, the debate will become outdated as new generations of children enter our schools having had increasing exposure to ICT in the home environment.

Teachers are already finding that the increasing numbers of computers and hi-tech devices in the home are resulting in children entering the education system with a whole range of ICT experience. A three-year-old at ease with a computer or digital camera is not unusual. However, at the other end of the spectrum, for some children ICT is a whole new area to explore.

The National Curriculum

The Foundation Stage of primary education accommodates children aged three to the end of the Reception year. The National Curriculum (2000) introduced the Foundation Stage in September 2000 and incorporates six key areas of learning:

- personal, social and emotional development
- communication, language and literacy
- mathematical development
- knowledge and understanding of the world
- physical development
- creative development.

The inclusion of ICT within these areas is defined by the early learning goals for ICT, which have two clear objectives:

- children need to be made aware of and be able to identify everyday technology

- children need to use ICT to support learning.

It is generally accepted that throughout the Foundation Stage children should be encouraged to use ICT as a tool to enhance their learning experience through the specified areas of learning.

Linking the early learning goals for ICT to the areas of learning

There are many ways in which ICT can enhance the specified areas of learning. This section takes each area of learning in turn and provides a brief overview of the benefits that the integration of ICT can bring.

● Personal, social and emotional development

The majority of children enjoy interactive activities; integrating ICT into a session can motivate and excite children, increasing interest and focus. The use of ICT can also improve a child's confidence, self-esteem and increase their attention span.

ICT activities encourage collaboration, enabling children to explore ICT by working in pairs or small groups to develop their communication and social skills. By sharing these learning experiences the children are stimulated to demonstrate their achievements through discussion and class plenary sessions.

● Communication, language and literacy

Having the confidence and skills to communicate effectively is important throughout life and at this early stage ICT can certainly help to nurture those skills. ICT activities involving role play can be used to stimulate creativity, demonstrating that receiving and providing information enables communication. By working with ICT equipment such as telephones, voice recorders and digital video recorders children can further develop their communication skills. Language, literacy and reading skills can also be enhanced by exposure to interactive computer programs, online stories and rhymes as well as group sessions using electronic whiteboards.

● Mathematical development

Computer programs can be a fun and stimulating way to introduce and develop counting skills and the recognition of numbers. There is a host of sorting, matching and sequencing computer activities available designed to develop a sense of size, colour and shape as well as developing language such as 'bigger' and 'smaller'.

● Knowledge and understanding of the world

ICT can help children develop a sense of the world around them by using cameras and voice recorders to investigate and record their immediate environment. Simulations and computer programs can help them appreciate other geographical areas and environments, with older children beginning to explore the resources of the Internet. Children can start to consider the machines they come across every day and question how they work and what they do.

● **Physical development**

Although less immediately obvious, ICT can play an important part in physical development by raising awareness of health and body functions through computer programs in the context of 'all about me'. ICT activities can also be incorporated in playground sessions, particularly when learning about giving and receiving instructions and sorting techniques.

● **Creative development**

The majority of computer programs intended for this age group are designed to encourage creativity, allowing children to experiment with images, songs and music. ICT such as voice recorders and video or digital cameras can be used to record individual or group activities involving the creation of music, song and dance.

ICT in the context of the Foundation Stage

At this early stage ICT is more about information and communication than technology. Children need to clearly understand these terms before they move on to consider how technology impacts on the way they handle information and communication. Computers can certainly be used to aid this process but a couple of computers placed in the corner of the room is most definitely not ICT.

The QCA does not provide a scheme of work for the Foundation Stage; however, the scheme of work for Year 1 does suggest that certain tasks can be completed during the Reception year. Although it is not suggested that the scheme for Year 1 is followed in depth, the recommended topics can provide some guidance in preparing children for Key Stage 1 and form a structure when planning and assessing.

ICT skills

At this stage of development the majority of children readily adapt to controlling a mouse and using it to select an object. They also enjoy using a keyboard either in role play (a dummy keyboard) or as part of a computer activity. Even at this early stage it is important to encourage the correct hand positioning on the keyboard and mouse as well as ensuring that computer equipment is ergonomically placed, away from direct sun or reflective light with an adjustable chair to ensure the correct level for hand and eye positioning.

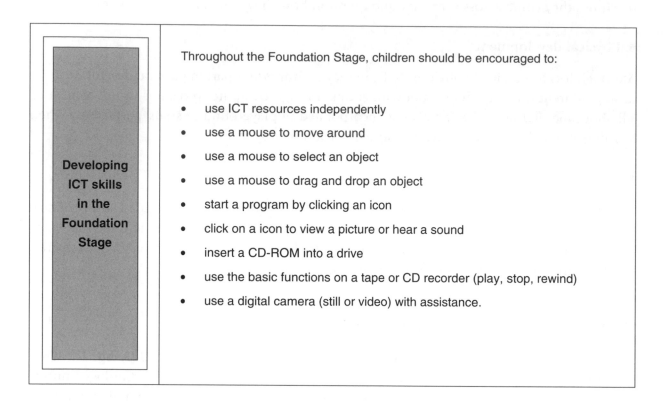

Throughout the Foundation Stage, children should be encouraged to:

Developing ICT skills in the Foundation Stage

- use ICT resources independently
- use a mouse to move around
- use a mouse to select an object
- use a mouse to drag and drop an object
- start a program by clicking an icon
- click on a icon to view a picture or hear a sound
- insert a CD-ROM into a drive
- use the basic functions on a tape or CD recorder (play, stop, rewind)
- use a digital camera (still or video) with assistance.

It is important to source a range of activities and games that develop mouse control and simple keyboard input. Make sure that all children have the opportunity to access computer equipment and develop these skills, particularly during the Reception year.

Aims and activities

The following activities provide the background experience, knowledge and skills required for Key Stage 1, while also considering the aims of the areas of learning and early learning goals for ICT, outlined for the Foundation Stage. Activities are loosely grouped under the areas of learning for the QCA scheme of work for Year 1 and it is worth spending some time looking at these ICT objectives before continuing (see Chapter 10). Suggestions for websites that can provide further examples of suitable activities are detailed at the end of this chapter.

Models – reality v fantasy

? What's it all about? At this stage of development imaginary play is an important part of the learning experience. Children enjoy role play and learn from copying the experiences and events they have witnessed themselves or through watching TV or another media. Toys, models and replicas play an important part in this development and for the older children computer simulations and games can take the experience a step further.

The aims The aim at this stage is to introduce the concept of a model. This can be achieved by comparing a toy to the 'real thing', for example a teddy to a real bear, a toy car to a real car. This can be extended to the comparison of a real event and an imaginary or fantasy event. Without taking away the joys of fantasy, the children can start to identify objects and situations that are not real.

Suggested activities

☞ Access the CBeebies section of the BBC website and choose any one of the characters displayed (Teletubbies, Fimbles, Pingu, Clifford, etc.). Engage the children in one of the selection of games or activities. Ask them whether the character is real (Have you ever met a Teletubby? Do you know anyone who has a dog like Clifford? Is Pingu a real penguin?).

☞ Organise a role-play activity (hospital, shop, office, etc.). Allow the children to dress up in appropriate costumes. Discuss the role play; are they a real doctor, nurse, shop assistant, etc.?

☞ Encourage the children to make a mask of an animal (provide paper plates or similar and appropriate art materials, fasten with elastic). Ask each child to act as their chosen animal (making the appropriate noise, action). Discuss the difference between the pretend and real animal.

☞ Cut out a series of pictures of animals from magazines. Cut the pictures of the animals into three: head, front legs and body, hind legs/tail. Provide the children with a pile of animal parts and encourage them to make a pretend animal by sticking random parts onto a sheet of paper. Access the Kinder Planet website and choose the Face on your egg game or Animal block puzzle for a similar online activity.

Communication – the written word

What's it all about? At Key Stage 1 this unit looks to develop a child's skill in selecting an appropriate word from a computerised word bank. At this stage, however, the important concept is the understanding that a word is used to convey information.

The aims The aim is to introduce the idea that the printed word has meaning and that words can be used to communicate. The children learn that 'things' have names and that a word can describe an object, an experience or a feeling.

Suggested activities

☞ Regularly use flash cards to help the children identify common objects. Start off with the type that has the object name written on the card and progress to matching cards with the picture on one card and the name on another.

☞ Use labels wherever possible; encourage the children to help you label wall displays, objects on the display tables, names on pegs, etc. Refer to the labels frequently.

☞ Familiar things like numbers and colours can also be identified as words. Play a game where either colours or numbers (as words) are displayed around the playground. Start off by holding up and reading out a card with the word that represents the colour or the number (red, blue, two, four, etc.). The children should run to the area of the playground with that number or colour displayed. As confidence increases just hold up the card and only read the word if necessary.

☞ Print out a keyboard template from the Northerngrid site and help the children colour the keys that make up their name. Help them type and print their name using a computer.

Information – using words, pictures and sounds

What's it all about? In Year 1 the children will start to consider that information can be presented using a mixture of media but at this stage it is important that children recognise that, in addition to words, pictures and sounds can provide information and aid communication.

The aims The aim is to help children understand that pictures and sounds tell them something; they provide information. Sounds such as the siren of a police car, the tune of an ice-cream van, the cry of a baby or the barking of a dog all provide information (the police car is in a hurry, the baby is hungry or tired, etc.). We can also identify things by sound; a dog barks, a cat meows. Pictures also provide information; they allow us to see things we may otherwise not see (a place in another country, the surface of the moon, a person we have never met).

Suggested activities

☞ Match the sound to the animal. Access the Fisher Price US site and select Fun & family time and then choose Fun & games, online! Choose the Animal sounds game from the Toddler's section.

☞ Allow the children to take a photo using a digital camera. Help them to print the photo. Make a wall display and ask the children to point out themselves or their friends. How do they recognise their friend; how do you know that is Lali? Because she has long black hair.

☞ Take the children on a walk around the school grounds or further afield. Listen to the sounds; what can they hear, do they know what it is from the sound (traffic, a bird singing)? What information does the sound provide?

☞ Show the children a picture that includes lots of information such as a busy street scene. Ask the children about the picture; what number is the bus, what is the weather like, how many people are at the bus stop? The aim is to encourage the children to glean information from a visual representation.

☞ Throughout the Foundation Stage use videos and DVDs (ICT) to show children places and activities that are new to them. Point out that the pictures they see, words and sounds they hear are all providing information.

Identifying, sorting and matching

 What's it all about?
At this stage labelling and classifying can be introduced by encouraging children to identify objects by using keywords; a ball is round, a car is red, a girl has brown hair. This can be extended with the older children to sorting objects based on size, colour or shape.

The aims
The aim is to encourage children to use words to describe the things they see around them (the teddy is brown, big). Taking this a stage further they can then start to identify an object by the information they receive (pass me the blue brick). These skills can then be developed to sort and match objects.

Suggested activities

☞ Encourage play with a model farm or zoo. Ask the children to put all the pigs into one pen, the cows in another, etc. Ask them how they decided what animal should go in what pen. Expand on answers such as 'because it's a pig' by asking how they know it is a pig (it's pink, has a curly tail, etc.).

☞ Use every opportunity to encourage children to sort and count objects (bricks, toys, playground equipment) based on colour, size, shape or type. Progress to sequencing the objects, largest to smallest.

☞ Create an autumn table displaying leaves, conkers, etc. Encourage the children to sort them and help them produce labels.

☞ Play 'snap' using a range of resources from standard snap cards to pairs of photos of the children in the class. Access the Kinder Planet site and select the Animated matching game to help the children develop their matching skills.

Visually representing information

What's it all about?   Even at this early stage children are receptive to visual representations of data. A wall display as a pictogram (favourite colour, means of travel to school) will provide interest in both the creation of the display and the exploration of the collected data.

The aims   The aim is to encourage children to start to interpret data. Children can identify the biggest and the smallest column on a pictogram, with older children starting to make comparisons and use terms such as more and less. There is also scope to include activities that involve recognising numbers and counting skills.

Suggested activities

☞   Provide a cut out picture of a teddy (or similar) and ask the children to colour the picture using their favourite colour (provide no more than five different coloured crayons). Use the pictures to produce a pictogram. Question the children about the data; which is the favourite colour, how do you know this, how many children like blue best?

☞   As an alternative to the colour pictogram, create a pictogram based on the children's favourite nursery rhyme. Use an electronic whiteboard and access the Smart Central or CBeebies websites for a range of rhymes; select 4 or 5. Ask the children to choose their favourite and draw a picture to represent the nursery rhyme. Use the pictures to create a wall display pictogram.

☞   For older children, provide a sheet of paper divided into five sections labelled Monday to Friday. Each morning ask the children to draw the sun, white cloud or black (rain) cloud depending on the weather. At the end of the week look back at the week and ask questions such as was it sunny on Wednesday, what was the weather like on Monday, how many days was it sunny this week?

The importance of instructions

 What's it all about? From an early age children realise that by pressing a button something happens; they can turn on the TV, change the channel using a remote or press the button on a camera to take a picture. They also start to become aware that the sequence of instructions has an importance: putting water in the kettle before switching it on or putting the dry pasta in the shaker before sealing the lid.

The aims At this stage children need to be encouraged to develop their listening skills so that they can successfully follow instructions. Simple directional and creative tasks can hone these skills while developing an awareness of the importance of following instructions.

Suggested activities

☞ Access the Fisher Price US site and select Fun & family time and then choose Fun & games. online! Select the Toddler games and locate the Discovery airport game. This game requires the children to use the mouse to negotiate a maze.

☞ Produce a simple treasure hunt or trail around the playground. Provide clear instructions on how to complete the challenge.

☞ Encourage the children to play board games such as Snakes and Ladders and Frustration. Help them to follow instructions when introducing playground games that are new to them.

☞ Use creative activities to reinforce the importance of instructions. Provide instructions on how to either grow something, such as a bulb, cress or a bean, or make something such as a musical instrument, cakes or biscuits.

☞ Encourage children to identify machines. Look at the machines in the classroom and around the school. Cut out some pictures of machines found in the home and produce a display. On trips outside of school, notice machines such as cars, lorries, traffic lights. Encourage role play with toy or 'dummy' machines such as computers, telephones and cookers. Consider how the machines can be turned off and on.

Assessment

The government states that a Foundation Stage Profile must be produced for each child by the end of the last term in the Reception year. The Foundation Stage Profile is used to summarise a child's progress and identify their learning needs at the end of the Foundation Stage. The information is based on observations and assessments made throughout the nursery and reception years. Recording a child's progress in using ICT should form a part of this general assessment.

Useful websites

CBeebies	www.bbc.co.uk/cbeebies
Fisher Price US	http://www.fisher-price.com/us/
Kinder Planet	www.kinderplanet.com/online.htm
Northerngrid	www.northerngrid.org/ngflwebsite/cjearlyyears/ EarlyYears/ICTearlyyearsskills.htm
Smart Central	www.smart-central.com

A further selection of useful websites can be found in Appendix B.

CHAPTER 10

Key Stage 1

This chapter is designed for those teaching children within Key Stage 1, Years 1 and 2 of primary education (ages 5 to 7). The sections cover the following areas:

- the National Curriculum for ICT for the key stage
- the QCA scheme of work for each year
- the ICT skills the children should have at the beginning of the school year
- the ICT experiences they should have participated in
- ways in which ICT can be integrated into core and year-specific subjects (including suggestions for activities)
- assessment.

National Curriculum

The National Curriculum for ICT at Key Stage 1 states that pupils should be taught knowledge, skills and understanding through:

- ❏ working with a range of information to investigate the different ways it can be presented

- ❏ exploring a variety of ICT tools

- ❏ talking about the uses of ICT inside and outside school.

The defined outcomes are detailed under the following four headings:

- ❏ Finding things out

- ❏ Developing ideas and making things happen

- ❏ Exchanging and sharing information

- ❏ Reviewing, modifying and evaluating work as it progresses.

QCA

The QCA schemes of work are comprehensive resources designed to help teachers translate the National Curriculum into workable classroom sessions. Schools are not obliged to use the QCA schemes but many do as they provide a sensible and adaptable structure to work from. The QCA scheme of work for Key Stage 1 suggests that ICT is incorporated into the curriculum through activities that cover the following areas of learning:

Year 1	Year 2
An introduction to modelling	Writing stories: communicating information using text
Using a word bank	Creating pictures
The information around us	Finding information
Labelling and classifying	Routes: controlling a floor turtle
Representing information graphically: pictograms	Questions and answers
Understanding instructions and making things happen	

Year 1

Year 1 class teachers and support staff should spend some time reading the previous chapter before moving on. This will provide familiarisation with the areas of ICT experienced by children during the early years and provide suggestions for suitable activities for those children needing some help and practice before moving on to the ICT-related activities within Key Stage 1.

Benchmarking

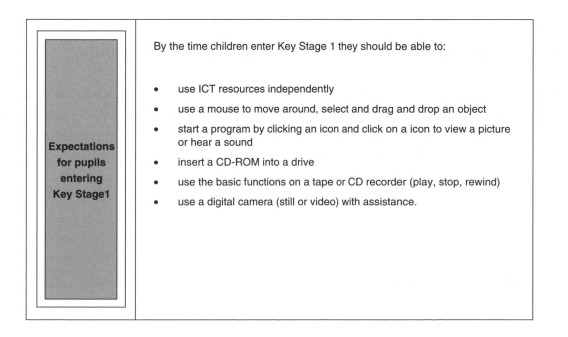

Expectations for pupils entering Key Stage 1

By the time children enter Key Stage 1 they should be able to:

- use ICT resources independently
- use a mouse to move around, select and drag and drop an object
- start a program by clicking an icon and click on a icon to view a picture or hear a sound
- insert a CD-ROM into a drive
- use the basic functions on a tape or CD recorder (play, stop, rewind)
- use a digital camera (still or video) with assistance.

ACTIVITY

It is well worth including a session at the beginning of Year 1 to benchmark the ICT knowledge/expertise of the children. This will help you plan future sessions and define groups for practical sessions. It will also help you to assess progress at the end of the year. Use some of the activities outlined in the previous chapter as a basis for this assessment. Record the starting point for each child using a spreadsheet or similar and add details of your observations throughout the year.

Developing ICT skills in Year 1

During Year 1, children develop their ICT skills by:

- using the mouse to position the cursor and move and place objects accurately on the screen
- becoming familiar with the keyboard and typing simple words
- using a word bank
- using basic drawing tools to create pictures
- adding clipart and pictures to their work
- creating a simple pictogram
- saving and printing work
- using a voice recorder.

ICT skills

Suggestions for ways to integrate ICT into the Year 1 curriculum

The following suggestions for activities are based on the QCA scheme of work for Year 1. This scheme provides guidelines for the areas of ICT development that should be addressed throughout the year. It is not necessary to follow any particular order; it is more important to be aware of the requirements and incorporate them into sessions as and when appropriate.

1A – An introduction to modelling

? What's it all about?

This unit is designed to show children that ICT can be used to represent both real and imaginary situations. TV, videos, DVDs and computers can all be used to provide information as sounds and pictures. Some of this information is real (the news, documentaries, nature programmes) and other information is fantasy (cartoons, computer games).

◉ The aims

It is often difficult for a child to differentiate between a real and imaginary situation. The aim of this unit is to gradually introduce activities that make children question and ultimately recognise the difference between 'real' and 'pretend'. This can be achieved in many ways and should be a year-long objective rather than a few directed activities. Comparing toys, representations made by the children (pictures, models) and computer games/simulations with the 'real thing' will help a child to gradually develop an understanding of this concept. This unit can be integrated into art and design, DT and literacy sessions.

 Keywords

Real, Fantasy, Imaginary, Pretend

Suggested activities

☞ Encourage the children to differentiate between real and pretend food. As a class or in groups make a model birthday cake that can be used to celebrate birthdays, make cakes using sand or modelling clay and make 'real' cakes (rice crispie cakes are an easy choice).

☞ Using a digital camera, allow the children to take a portrait photograph of their partner. Use these digital portraits as a basis for drawing or painting a self-portrait. Compare the 'real' image of the photograph to the representation.

☞ When playing with toys (cars, dolls, teddies, farm or zoo animals) ask the children how the toy compares to the real thing.

☞ Show an example of a cartoon or film using a DVD and electronic whiteboard. Explore how the characters differ from real people and animals. As an alternative, access the Little Critter website for examples of animated animals.

☞ Read the children a range of fairy stories and stories about fantasy worlds. Discuss each story and reinforce the ICT objective to distinguish between reality and fantasy.

1B – Using a word bank

What's it all about? This unit is designed to introduce word-processing software and specifically the word bank feature that is available with many of the word-processing packages designed for primary level. The unit also provides an opportunity for children to gain a basic awareness of the keyboard or consolidate skills developed during the Foundation Stage.

The aims The aim is to gradually introduce computers as a means of creating a simple sentence, building on the concept that words convey information. Children increase their exposure to the written word using computerised word banks and picture banks.

Keywords Information, Style, Font, Word bank, Picture bank

Suggested activities

☞ Reinforce the importance of words. Ask the children to find examples of words that provide information in their classroom. Help them to identify signs, labels, captions, lists and instructions.

☞ Using an electronic whiteboard remind the children of the layout of the letters on the computer keyboard; point out the vowels. Ask the children if they have a vowel in their name. Access the Fun School website and select the Letter matching game (or similar) to reinforce. As an extension activity access the BBC schools website and locate the creamcake word bank rhyming exercise.

☞ Use keyboard activities to help reinforce the use of high frequency words for Year 1. Use word-processing software such as Textease CT to create word banks and simple sentences. Also use picture banks to illustrate the text.

1C – The information around us

? **What's it all about?** This unit is designed to increase awareness of the information that is all around us. Information can be presented as words, sounds, pictures or a combination of these media. Children are introduced to the concept of multimedia and the fact that different media can be used for different purposes.

◉ **The aims** The aim is to encourage children to use different media when communicating or presenting information. Activities should be ongoing throughout the year, concentrating on the identification of sources of information and consideration of the way in which the information is presented. Children are encouraged to present their work in different ways, including the use of ICT such as digital cameras, voice recorders and printouts from computer activities. This unit can be linked to literacy and science.

⚷ **Keywords** Information, Sound, Picture, Text, Media, Multimedia

Suggested activities

☞ Remind the children that words provide information. Use some of the examples from previous activities.

☞ Introduce the idea that sounds provide information by using the Sound Monster word bank activity on the BBC schools website. Recap on the different sounds that provide information such as a police siren, ice-cream van chimes, someone crying or laughing.

☞ Introduce the idea that pictures provide information. Show the children two books, one with illustrations and one without. Discuss the differences. Encourage the children to use a multimedia computer package such as 2Create a Story (see Chapter 5) to produce a simple animated story. This is a multimedia presentation tool that incorporates words, pictures and sounds.

☞ Use a sound recorder to record the children talking about an activity they have participated in. This can be used as part of a classroom display. For example, the children can produce an autumnal wall display and record their experiences of collecting or creating the objects for the display. This recording can be played alongside the display at a parents' event. Expand this activity to include photographs or video footage of the children to enhance the presentation.

1D – Labelling and classifying

What's it all about? This unit builds on the idea that objects can be described and identified by the use of keywords. Initially this involves the shape, colour or size of the object (the blue car, big ball, round brick) leading on to more complex descriptions using more than one keyword (the big bear with brown fur and red coat). Once this concept has been grasped activities can move on to considering sorting and sequencing based on criteria (sort the bricks into three piles based on colour; put the bears in line, smallest first).

The aims The aim is to show the children that they can identify an object based on the information provided. This skill, along with the development of descriptive language, is required across the curriculum with sorting and sequencing skills playing an important part in numeracy and science.

Keywords Information, Keyword, Describe, Sort, Sequence, Group

Suggested activities

☞ Recap on the use of descriptive vocabulary by asking the children to describe objects. Display a range of objects on a table and ask the children to look at them. Ask the children to turn away from the table and take one of the objects, describing it to the children. Can they identify it? This activity aids memory as well as listening skills.

☞ Using a large bag of coloured bricks ask the children to sort the bricks based on given criteria such as size, colour or shape. Introduce language to describe 3-D shapes and develop counting skills using the piles of bricks. Encourage comparisons such as this pile is the biggest, there are more bricks in this pile.

☞ Access the Longman website and select What are they wearing? and Who is it? Use these activities for ideas or adaptation. Alternatively use the popular Guess Who? board game (MB games). All these activities require the children to identify a person based on characteristics such as hair colour, hair length, clothes.

☞ Access the Fun School website and select the Clean up your world activity. This sorting game requires the children to recycle by placing rubbish in the correct bins.

☞ Practise sequencing skills by accessing the Paw Park Alphabet Bears activity at the Cogcon website. This activity involves alphabet sequencing.

1E – Representing information graphically: pictograms

What's it all about? This unit introduces the idea that information can be more accessible when represented visually. This is demonstrated through simple pictograms created both manually and by using a computer program.

The aims The aim is for children to create pictograms and actively draw inferences and conclusions from the data. This can be linked to activities across the curriculum including numeracy, science and geography.

Keywords Data/Information, Pictogram, Collect, Sort, Classify

Suggested activities

☞ Introduce pictograms by producing a manual variety. Carry out a simple survey such as favourite chocolate bar, colour, means of travelling to school. Where possible link this into a current class activity and make sure that the choices are limited. For example, linking it to literacy, play (or read) 4 or 5 fairy stories to the children (online varieties can be found at the BBC CBeebies website). Ask the children to choose their favourite and draw a picture to represent the story. Use these pictures to create a pictogram wall display. Encourage the development of counting and comparison skills; 3 children liked Snow White best, more children liked Cinderella than Snow White.

☞ Using similar data to the examples provided for the manual exercise, create simple pictograms using a suitable software program (see Chapter 6).

1F – Understanding instructions and making things happen

What's it all about? This unit is designed to introduce the importance of clear and accurate instructions. Activities consider the instructions needed to control everyday appliances and machines as well as the instructions that people need to complete a task.

The aims The aim is to help children appreciate the importance of giving and receiving clear and accurate instruction. This can involve the instructions given when making something, when playing a game or travelling to a location (a place in the playground or another room in the school). This involves the development of listening, communication and comprehension skills as well as an appreciation of the need to provide instructions in the correct sequence.

Children are also shown how machines follow instructions, some simple and others more complex. Taking a selection of machines that can be found in the school or at home, the children learn to appreciate that machines need to be turned on and off and some machines need further instruction for them to operate.

Keywords Control, Sequence, Order, Instruction

Suggested activities

☞ Introduce the importance of following instructions by playing a selection of games such as the playground games 'Simon says' or 'What's the time, Mr Wolf?' and board games like Snakes and Ladders or Frustration. Stress the importance of listening carefully to the instructions before starting the game. This can be reinforced by playing the Bingo game from the Longman website.

☞ Reinforce the importance of following instructions by making something. Link this to a current activity, for example making musical instruments (music), growing a bean or a bulb (science). Alternatively use the Gingerbread Boy Story from the Longman website and follow the instructions to make the puppet using the template. The activity is accompanied by an audio story.

☞ Consider machines and the instructions needed to make them work. Linking to a current activity, help the children make a voice or video recording (singing, dancing, drama or just a play activity). The emphasis is on making the equipment work, switching it on and off and, if necessary, rewinding and replaying.

☞ Look at other machines that can be found in the school and surrounding areas. Take a trip to the school office for a demonstration of a photocopier; notice the machines on the road outside the school (car, bus, lorry, traffic lights, barrier). Talk about machines found at home (cooker, fridge, TV, video). Make a collage of pictures from machines using old magazines.

Year 2

By Year 2 confidence is growing and the inconsistencies of experience through pre-school exposure to ICT should be less of a issue.

Benchmarking

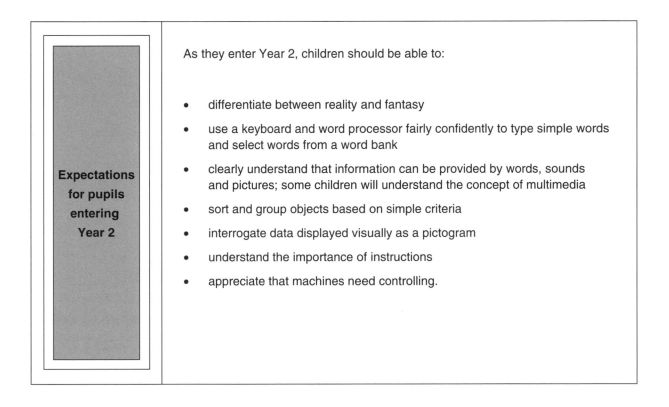

	As they enter Year 2, children should be able to:
Expectations for pupils entering Year 2	• differentiate between reality and fantasy • use a keyboard and word processor fairly confidently to type simple words and select words from a word bank • clearly understand that information can be provided by words, sounds and pictures; some children will understand the concept of multimedia • sort and group objects based on simple criteria • interrogate data displayed visually as a pictogram • understand the importance of instructions • appreciate that machines need controlling.

ACTIVITY

You may choose to carry out a number of simple activities at the beginning of the year to assess knowledge and expertise. It is suggested that you do this by adapting a few of the more general tasks carried out in Year 1 or by designing an integrated activity to encompass a range of skills. Note the individual abilities of the children on a spreadsheet or similar and keep a record of progress throughout the year.

ICT skills

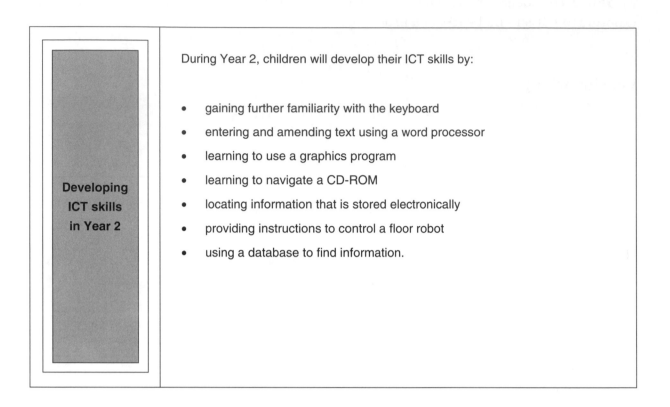

Developing ICT skills in Year 2	During Year 2, children will develop their ICT skills by:
	• gaining further familiarity with the keyboard
	• entering and amending text using a word processor
	• learning to use a graphics program
	• learning to navigate a CD-ROM
	• locating information that is stored electronically
	• providing instructions to control a floor robot
	• using a database to find information.

Suggestions for ways to integrate ICT into the Year 2 curriculum

The Year 2 QCA scheme of work for ICT provides opportunities to increase word-processing skills as well as introducing data handling and the first elements of control.

2A – Writing stories: communicating information using text

What's it all about? This unit is designed to continue the theme that the written word conveys information. This unit takes this idea a stage further by considering the importance of clarity and punctuation.

The aims Children are encouraged to experiment with word processing and are taught basic punctuation such as adding spaces, using the Shift, Backspace and Enter/Return keys. Using the word processor to create stories, they learn how to save text and amend it at a later date.

Once these basic skills have been learned, the children should be encouraged to use the word processor on a regular basis when producing textual documents, although not to the detriment of developing handwriting skills. Children should frequently be shown how to position their hands correctly on the keyboard and encouraged to develop touch-typing skills. The ICT skills should be developed alongside literacy skills throughout the year.

Keywords Word processor, Cursor, Shift, Backspace, Edit

Suggested activities

☞ As punctuation skills are introduced and practised during literacy sessions use a mixture of handwriting and word-processing activities for reinforcement. Gradually introduce the different keys through suitable exercises. For example:

❑ Create a document with spaces missing between words and show the children how to insert a space.
❑ Create a document with some errors and show the children how to use the Backspace key.
❑ Create a document without capitalisation and show the children how to use the Shift key.

☞ Point out the benefits of being able to edit the word-processed document. Talk about how much easier it is to make changes and correct mistakes (compare with using an eraser or crossing out).

2B – Creating pictures

 What's it all about?   This unit is designed to encourage children to use ICT to develop visual ideas. Using a graphics program they can produce simple drawings that can be saved and then enhanced.

 The aims   Children are shown how to use the simple tools of a graphics program to draw and fill with colour. They are encouraged to experiment with a range of techniques and compare the results with pictures created by hand.

Once these basic skills have been practised the children can use ICT to produce pictures for a whole range of applications, such as illustrating stories (hand written or word processed) or any other cross-curricular activity that requires illustration. This unit is all about experimentation and having fun with computer graphics; however, it is important not to use ICT tools to the exclusion of developing those skills required for drawing or painting by hand. The aim is to complete tasks using both methods and then compare the results. This unit has obvious links to the curricula activities for art and design.

Keywords   Graphics, Image, Palette, Tools

Suggested activities

☞ Show the children how to use the basic features of a graphics package (see Chapter 7). Draw simple shapes using the available tools and then use the fill tools to add colour. Allow time for the children to experiment.

☞ Access the All Posters website and use the search box to search for Pollock (to find examples of paintings by Jackson Pollock). Use an electronic whiteboard to display a selection of the paintings (they feature seemingly abstract shapes and colours with splashes and spots). Ask the children for their opinions and print out and display some of their favourites. Set them the task of producing a 'Pollock' style painting firstly using traditional methods and then using a computer package. Discuss the results and compare the process.

☞ Access the All Posters website and use the search box to search for Mondrian (to find examples of paintings by Piet Mondrian). Use an electronic whiteboard to display a selection of the paintings (they feature geometric shapes, horizontal and vertical lines and primary colours). Ask the children for their opinions and print out and display some of their favourites. Set them the task of producing a 'Mondrian' style painting firstly using traditional methods and then using a computer package. Discuss the results and compare the process. Compare the Pollock and Mondrian styles; which do they prefer, which was easier to produce?

2C – Finding information

What's it all about?   This unit is designed to enable children to discover the whole range of exciting cross-curricular information available on CD-ROM and the World Wide Web.

The aims   Children are shown how to move around the pages of information held on an information-based CD-ROM (such as a CD-ROM containing a number of stories or factual information) and use keywords to locate information. Alternatively, use a suitable website for these activities. This can be compared with manually finding information using the contents page or index of a book, meeting cross-curricular objectives for literacy.

Keywords   CD-ROM, Contents, Index, Menu

Suggested activities

☞   Within a literacy session introduce the children to the navigation features available with books. Consider the way that a book is broken down into chapters, with a contents page at the front providing a list of the chapters and the page number on which they start. Show the children an index and explain how to use it.

☞   Relate the navigational features of a book to a CD-ROM. Explain that a CD-ROM can contain the information of many books; in fact a CD-ROM can hold the same amount of words as around 1,000 novels (and it takes up much less shelf space). Use a CD-ROM encyclopaedia such as Encarta. Introduce the ideas of menus and buttons to move around. Search for a topic that is relevant to current history or geography sessions. Allow the children to move around and experiment with the links. As an alternative to a CD-ROM access the KidsClick! website for a child-friendly information site with all the features of a CD-ROM encyclopaedia.

2D – Routes: controlling a floor turtle

What's it all about? This unit follows on from activities involving the giving and receiving of instructions covered in Year 1 and is designed to introduce the concept of programming. The need to give machines instructions is demonstrated using a floor robot or programmable toy.

The aims Children are shown how to give instructions to control the robot and are encouraged to repeat sequences and predict outcomes. This unit has direct links to cross-curricular objectives for numeracy, particularly around the areas of shape and space, number sequences and measures. Children increase their mathematical vocabulary by describing position, direction and movement.

Keywords Floor robot, Control device, Instructions, Program

Suggested activities

☞ Make sure that the children understand how to give and receive simple instructions for moving around. Choose a location with either a tiled or paved floor (paving slabs). Encourage the children to give each other instructions such as forward 5, left 2, back 3 (you will need to set the rules and demonstrate, i.e. when going left, side step to the left so still facing the same direction). Introduce a target destination and ask the children to give instructions to reach it.

☞ You may feel it helpful to reinforce these skills by using a series of maze puzzles; printable examples can be found at the ABC Teach website. Again, encourage the use of directional language.

☞ If you have a Roamer turtle, access the Kent NGfL website for some suggestions on activities suitable for this year group. See Chapter 8 for further references to sites that provide instructions on using floor turtles and similar devices.

2E – Questions and answers

What's it all about? This unit is designed to enable children to analyse information by developing questioning techniques and predicting responses. By developing an understanding of the difference between open and closed questions children can start to develop their questioning skills through practical activities.

The aims Through activities children learn the uses and limitations of asking closed questions, questions where the answer can either be yes or no. This is extended to looking at open questions and the type of information that can be found particularly through the use of computer databases. The development of these skills can be linked to literacy, numeracy and science.

Keywords Information, Data, Sort, Classify, Questionnaire, Database, Record, Field

Suggested activities

☞ Remind the children about descriptive words. Take a small group of children and play 'pass the parcel' with different, interesting objects. Each time the music stops, the child holding the object provides a word to describe the object (that hasn't already been given).

☞ Get the children used to closed questions by playing the yes/no game. Use a set of pictures of animals (cat, dog, pig, cow, etc.), or similar. Ask a child to choose a picture but not show it to you. Ask yes/no questions to identify the animal; does it have fur, does it bark, do you get milk from it? When the children have the idea let them play the game in pairs. Playing the Guess Who? game (from MB games) can reinforce this. Create a branching database to demonstrate the animal yes/no game. Display it on the electronic whiteboard, asking the children the questions and following the routes through the tree.

☞ Create a pictogram based on hair colour (either manually or using a suitable computer package). Collecting the data for this activity requires a yes/no question. Do you have blonde/black/brown/red hair? Question the data; how many children have brown hair, what is the most/least common hair colour? Take it a step further and look at the limitations of this type of information display. Ask, does the pictogram show us what colour hair Joe has? Does it show us if most blonde-haired children have blue or brown eyes?

☞ Create a very simple database using a suitable software package. Enter name, hair colour and eye colour (and include a picture if your software allows). Show the children how to question this data and introduce the terms database, record and field.

End of key stage assessment

Focus has moved away from formal written tests at the end of Key Stage 1 towards teacher assessment. This is usually carried out as an ongoing activity throughout the two years, with the Year 1 teacher providing an update as part of the transition from Year 1 to Year 2. Although ICT does not feature as part of this assessment it is helpful to provide an ICT-key stage assessment for each child that can be passed on to the Year 3 teacher.

Useful websites

ABC Teach	www.abcteach.com/directory/fun_activities/maze_fun/
All Posters	www.allposters.co.uk
BBC CBeebies	www.bbc.co.uk/cbeebies/storycircle/fairystories/
BBC schools	www.bbc.co.uk/schools/magickey/adventures/creamcake.shtml
BBC schools	www.bbc.co.uk/schools/magickey/adventures/soundmonster_game.shtml
Cogcon	www.cogcon.com/gamegoo/gooey.html
Fun School	www.funschool.com
Kent NGfL	www.kented.org.uk/NGfL/ict/robots/games.html
Kidsclick!	http://sunsite.berkeley.edu/KidsClick%21/
Longman	www.longman.com/young_learners/teachers/resources-archive/
Little Critter	www.littlecritter.com

CHAPTER 11

Key Stage 2

> This chapter is designed for those teaching children within Key Stage 2, Years 3 to 6 of primary education (ages 7 to 11). The sections cover the following areas:

- ❑ the National Curriculum for ICT for the key stage
- ❑ the QCA scheme of work for each year
- ❑ the ICT skills the children should have at the beginning of the school year
- ❑ the ICT experiences they should have participated in
- ❑ ways in which ICT can be integrated into core and year specific subjects (including suggestions for activities)
- ❑ assessment.

National Curriculum

The National Curriculum for ICT states that during Key Stage 2 pupils should:

- ❑ use a wider range of ICT tools and information sources to support their work in other subjects
- ❑ develop their research skills and decide what information is appropriate for their work
- ❑ begin to question the plausibility and quality of information
- ❑ learn how to amend their work and present it in a way that suits its audience.

The knowledge, skills and understanding required to achieve this are defined as:

- ❑ Finding things out

- ❑ Developing ideas and making things happen

- ❑ Exchanging and sharing information

- ❑ Reviewing, modifying and evaluating work as it progresses.

QCA

The National Curriculum for ICT at Key Stage 2 is comprehensive and covers a four-year period of development. To provide some structure the QCA schemes of work offer suggestions on ways in which the National Curriculum can be translated into year-by-year objectives and workable classroom sessions. Schools are not obliged to use the QCA schemes but many do as they provide a sensible and adaptable structure to work from. The QCA schemes of work for Key Stage 2 suggest that ICT is incorporated into the curriculum through activities that cover the following areas of learning:

Year 3	Year 4
Combining text and graphics	Writing for different audiences
Manipulating sound	Developing images using repeating patterns
Introduction to databases	Branching databases
Exploring simulations	Collecting and presenting information: questionnaires and pie charts
E-mail	Modelling effects on screen
Year 5	**Year 6**
Graphical modelling	Multimedia presentation
Analysing data and asking questions using complex searches	Spreadsheet modelling
Evaluating information, checking accuracy and questioning plausibility	Control and monitoring – What happens when …?
Introduction to spreadsheets	Using the Internet to search large databases and to interpret information
Controlling devices	
Monitoring environmental conditions and changes	

Year 3

It is suggested that Year 3 teachers take some time to read the previous chapter outlining the ICT experience and skills that children attain during Key Stage 1.

Benchmarking

By the time children reach Key Stage 2 they should view ICT as a natural part of their classroom activities. The aim is to develop this confident approach to using ICT and promote the understanding that ICT is a tool to be used as and when appropriate.

Expectations for pupils entering Year 3

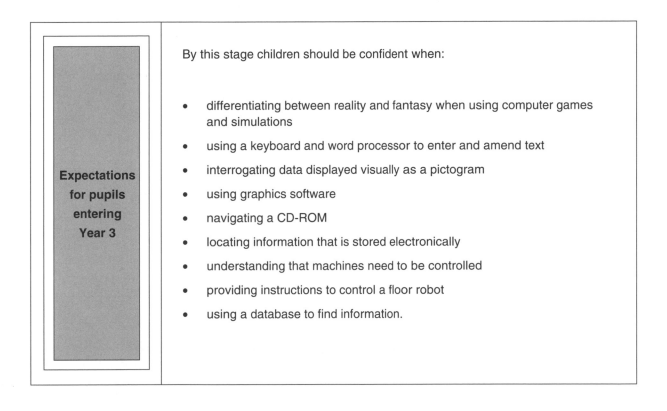

Expectations for pupils entering Year 3

By this stage children should be confident when:

- differentiating between reality and fantasy when using computer games and simulations
- using a keyboard and word processor to enter and amend text
- interrogating data displayed visually as a pictogram
- using graphics software
- navigating a CD-ROM
- locating information that is stored electronically
- understanding that machines need to be controlled
- providing instructions to control a floor robot
- using a database to find information.

ACTIVITY

The Year 3 teacher is provided with an overall view of a child's ability by means of the formal end of Key Stage 1 assessment. This assessment is not specific to ICT proficiency and you may choose to carry out a number of simple activities at the beginning of the year to assess the expected knowledge and expertise at this stage. It is suggested that you do this by adapting a few of the more general tasks carried out in Year 2 or by designing an integrated activity to encompass a range of skills. Make a note of individual abilities on a spreadsheet or similar and keep a record of the children's progress throughout the year.

ICT skills

Developing ICT skills in Years 3

<table>
<tr>
<td>Developing ICT skills in Year 3</td>
<td>

During Year 3, children develop their ICT skills by:

- working with text using fonts, colours and sizes
- working with pictures; loading from an external source, resizing
- combining text and graphics
- using a word processor to improve punctuation and varied vocabulary
- using a computer program to explore musical ideas
- using a recording machine to record musical sounds
- adding data to a database
- sorting and searching records in a database
- viewing, exploring and interacting with a computer simulation
- sending, receiving and responding to an e-mail message
- using an e-mail address book
- sending an e-mail with an attachment.
</td>
</tr>
</table>

Suggestions for ways to integrate ICT into the Year 3 curriculum

The ICT requirements for Year 3 are varied and stimulating. There is plenty of opportunity for the Year 3 teacher to integrate the development of these ICT skills into the general curriculum. The content strongly relates to literacy, numeracy, music and art and design, with opportunities to incorporate the simulation within a geography or history session and relate the use of databases to science activities.

3A – Combining text and graphics

What's it all about? This unit looks at ways in which a computer can be used to improve the layout and presentation of a document through both design and content. Design aspects include formatting, the use of colour and inclusion of pictures – features that make the document visually appealing and fit for purpose. Content issues include the use of punctuation and the choice of a varied vocabulary.

The aims Children are encouraged to produce visually appealing documents that successfully achieve an objective. For example, a poster that is colourful, eye-catching and easy to read or a newspaper article that has a headline that stands out and an interesting photograph that catches the attention of the reader. They are encouraged to consider punctuation and the use of capital letters as well as the actual content of the text. Emphasis is placed on reducing repetition by using a range of synonyms, for example using words to replace *nice* such as lovely, pleasing, beautiful. The word processor can then be used to make these changes by editing the document. This activity can be integrated within literacy sessions with a general awareness of using word processing to enhance documentation throughout the curriculum.

Keywords Font, Format, Edit, Synonym, Punctuation

Suggested activities

☞ Spend some time collecting and looking at visually appealing documents such as greetings cards, posters, adverts, newsletters and magazines. Consider what makes the documents attractive. Ask the children to produce a poster for a future school event (using traditional materials, paints, collage, etc.). Discuss the outcome with respect to use of colour, pictures and the size of text.

☞ Use a computer package to produce a document that has relevance to a current curricula topic. Look at altering font size, font type and colour. Demonstrate any available special effects such as the shimmering or sparkling text formats available with Microsoft Word (**Format, Font, Text effects**). Look at enhancing particular words such as typing the word rainbow with each letter a different colour or writing BIG *or* small to reflect the size. Ask the children for further suggestions. Encourage accurate and consistent punctuation.

☞ Introduce the use of synonyms to create more interesting and varied prose and rhymes. Use the synonym example sheet at the Primary Resources website to introduce the concept. Use the synonym computer activities at the Tiger Towson website as reinforcement.

Ask the children to provide as many different words as possible that can be used instead of 'said' (whispered, shouted, replied, gasped, etc.). Produce a short word-processed conversational document that uses 'said' throughout. Ask the children to edit the document using the word-processing software replacing 'said' with a range of alternatives.

☞ Produce a factual document (or ask the children to) based on a current topic such as one of the Year 3 science topics. Make the document more visually appealing by adding illustrations. Either use suitable clipart, copy pictures from the Internet, scan in pictures drawn by the children or use illustrations created by the children using a computer graphics package.

3B – Manipulating sound

What's it all about? This unit is designed to encourage children to develop a musical awareness by exploring music through both traditional methods and using a computer. ICT can also be used to record musical sessions and present compositions.

The aims Children are shown how to compose simple expressions using musical instruments and computer music software. Resulting compositions can be recorded and played back either as finished pieces or as backing tracks for live music sessions. This activity can be integrated within music sessions.

Keywords Timbre, String, Percussion, Woodwind, Sequence

Suggested activities

☞ Use an electronic keyboard to introduce the sounds made by different instruments. Produce a range of picture cards illustrating different instruments; as you play an instrument on the keyboard ask the children to identify and raise the picture of the correct instrument.

☞ Access the Play Music website and allow the children to listen to a whole range of orchestral instruments. For further links to music websites, access the excellent Coxhoe Primary School website.

☞ Use music software such as 2Simple Music Toolkit to produce simple musical expressions.

☞ Tape the musical expressions created by the children using the music software. Use this as a backing track when playing a selection of instruments. Use a digital camera to record the children's 'concert'.

3C – Introduction to databases

What's it all about? This unit reinforces the concept of a database and the associated terminology such as record and field. By comparing manual and computerised database systems, the children are made aware of the advantages of storing information electronically.

The aims Through the use of both paper and computerised databases the children are shown the advantages of storing data so that specific information can easily be found. The children sort data into order based on a given criterion such as displaying a given field alphabetically or numerically and are shown how to search for specific information based on criteria. This activity can be integrated within sessions involving the analysis of data.

Keywords Database, Record, Field, Sort, Criteria, Search

Suggested activites

☞ Get the children used to searching paper databases by using an example such as the telephone directory. Show the children how to use the directory and discuss the fact that the records are sorted in alphabetical order.

☞ Spend a week observing the weather and recording the information on record cards. Produce a batch of template record cards with the fieldnames Date, Day of week, Temperature, Sky type and the logical fields Rain? and Windy? At the same time each day, help the children fill in a card. With seven cards completed (include a weekend homework task) put the cards in date order. Ask the children some questions such as did it rain on Monday, on how many days was it windy, was there a blue sky, was the sky black/grey/white?

☞ Transfer the weather data to a computerised database. Create the structure and allow the children to add the records. Question the data in the same way as before. Create a simple graph to represent the data.

☞ Working in pairs or small groups, encourage the children to design a database to hold information about class members. For example, the fields could include name, age, boy/girl, height, eye colour, birthday month. Once designed help them collect the data using record cards and then create a computerised database and add the records. Query the data.

3D – Exploring simulations

What's it all about? This unit demonstrates the use of simulations to represent real or imaginary situations. By considering situations where a simulation is essential or beneficial, children start to appreciate the advantages of this facility.

The aims By showing children a number of simulations, either recorded on video/DVD or computer-generated simulations, they can evaluate the simulation and compare it to the real situation. The aim is for children to discover that there are some 'real' situations that they are never likely to experience and simulation is 'the next best thing'. By providing examples, the children can experience for themselves the advantages that simulation can bring. This unit has strong links to geography, history and science where the subject of discussion can often be intangible (computer simulations of historic battles, simulations showing the growth of a plant, simulation of the eruption of a volcano).

 Keywords Simulation, Evaluate

Suggested activities

☞ Talk about simulations, what they are and why they are used. Consider simulations used for learning: flight simulator, medical simulators used by surgeons, architectural simulators for design, and recreational simulations in the form of computer games. Computer simulations are designed to look real but they are simply imitating the real thing. Simulations are useful when it is too difficult, dangerous, costly or remote to do 'the real thing', for example learning to fly a plane, walking on the moon, climbing a mountain or designing a new building.

☞ Show some examples of computer simulations and allow the children to experiment. Access the Kent NGfL website for a range of simulations and look at the BBC website for a simulation of the weather (select the weather element such as cloud or cloud/rain and then click on the play button to the right of the controls). Search the Internet for simulations relevant to current topics.

3E – E-mail

| | **What's it all about?** | This unit considers communicating over a distance including historic as well as present methods. Emphasis is given to the use of e-mail: sending, receiving, responding, and sending attachments. Children are also encouraged to use an address book to record the e-mail addresses of friends and family. |

The aims — E-mail is introduced through the context of methods of communication. Children should be encouraged to use e-mail within a controlled environment, ideally with the opportunity to communicate with an 'e-mail pal' from another school. This does involve coordination but is well worth the time and effort it takes. This activity can be linked to general literacy skills involving written communication and to geography when considering 'Connecting ourselves to the world'.

Keywords — Communication, E-mail, E-mail address, Attachment

Suggested activities

☞ Look at the history of communication from smoke signals and the pony express through to communicating via e-mail and text messaging. Access the Inventors website and select The History of Communication for a useful overview.

☞ Link up with another school, preferably in a different area of the country (or another English-speaking country) and pair each child with an e-mail 'pen pal'. Encourage them to communicate regularly to gain familiarity with sending and receiving e-mails. Access the ePALS website to find a school to link with.

☞ Initiate a project that involves the children finding out about their e-mail pal and the area or country where they live. This will involve sending attachments with e-mails such as photographs or relevant documents.

Year 4

Year 4 involves a varied range of ICT learning objectives, all of which build on existing skills. This provides opportunity for consolidation, practice and development before the children move on to Year 5 and a number of new ICT concepts.

Benchmarking

By the time children reach Year 4 they have a broad overview of ICT and are ready to consolidate that learning and develop a deeper insight to its practical applications.

Expectations for pupils entering Year 4

Expectations for pupils entering Year 4	You should be able to assume that the children joining your class at the beginning of Year 4 have had experience in: • using a keyboard and word processor to enter and amend text; working with text using fonts, colours and sizes; using a word processor to improve punctuation and varied vocabulary • using a graphics program to produce a simple picture; working with pictures, loading from an external source, resizing, combining text and graphics • using a simple database; adding data to a database; sorting and searching records in a database; using a database to find information • interrogating data displayed visually as a pictogram • understanding that machines need to be controlled; providing instructions to control a floor robot.

ACTIVITY

The tasks for Year 4 build on these skills and it is advisable to start the year by ensuring that the children are competent in these areas. The Year 4 teacher should be provided with an assessment of each child's ICT ability as documented by their Year 3 teacher. You may choose to carry out a number of simple activities at the beginning of the year to check or assess this knowledge and expertise. It is suggested that you do this by adapting a few of the more general tasks carried out in previous years or by designing an integrated activity to encompass a range of skills. Make a note of the individual abilities of each child on a spreadsheet or similar and keep a record of progress throughout the year.

ICT skills

Developing ICT skills in Year 4

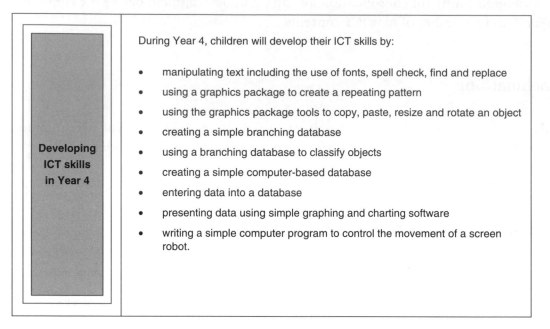

Developing ICT skills in Year 4	During Year 4, children will develop their ICT skills by: • manipulating text including the use of fonts, spell check, find and replace • using a graphics package to create a repeating pattern • using the graphics package tools to copy, paste, resize and rotate an object • creating a simple branching database • using a branching database to classify objects • creating a simple computer-based database • entering data into a database • presenting data using simple graphing and charting software • writing a simple computer program to control the movement of a screen robot.

Suggestions for ways to integrate ICT into the Year 4 curriculum

The Year 4 ICT topics are varied in nature but all have distinct links to other areas of the curriculum. The majority of the following suggested activities could be easily integrated into cross-curricular topics.

4A – Writing for different audiences

 What's it all about? This unit is designed to encourage children to consider style and content when producing written work. The editing and text manipulation features of a word processor can be used to help children arrange their ideas and organise the content of a document. They can check for accuracy by utilising spell-checking features and improve appearance and presentation by incorporating a range of font attributes.

 The aims Children are encouraged to consider the design aspects of documents and deciding whether they are 'fit for purpose'. These design considerations can then be incorporated into written work whether produced by hand or word processor. Through experience children learn to ensure that a document conveys the correct message to the target audience as well as being accurate and presented in a clear and interesting way. This skill development impacts on all areas of the curriculum involving the use of narrative and can be enhanced throughout the year.

Keywords Edit, Font, Spell check, Presentation, Find/Replace

Suggested activities

☞ Look at a range of publications including newspapers, magazines and teaching materials. Consider who they are aimed at and whether they are fit for purpose. Consider how a magazine designed for a child differs from a newspaper. Look at design aspects; consider how titles draw the eye and pictures break up text. Talk about 'over-formatting'; documents can be difficult to read with too many variations in style.

☞ Produce a news-sheet related to a current curriculum subject. Each topic should have a title; the text should all be the same size, font and colour, with each topic separated by a blank line. Using a word processor ask the children to improve the look of the document by using different fonts, size of text and colour. Provide a picture bank with a range of relevant pictures. Remind the children to moderate the formatting or their document will become difficult to read.

☞ Demonstrate how to use a word processor to cut and paste text. Linking to science, produce a list of animals and below a list of habitats and/or information relevant to a specific animal. The second list should not be in the same order as the first. Ask the children to use the cut and paste techniques they have learnt to merge the two lists so that each paragraph includes an animal's name followed by the details concerning that animal.

☞ Throughout the year encourage children to use the word processor to produce documents. Demonstrate and assist the children with editing techniques such as using the Delete key, Backspace, overwrite/insert feature and the undo facility. Show them how to use the spell checker and remind them of the use of the thesaurus. Use the find and replace option if and when relevant.

4B – Developing images using repeating patterns

What's it all about? This unit is all about developing children's visual ideas. Whether through manual processes, or the use of a graphics package, the children are shown how repeated images can become building blocks for larger pictures. Children are encouraged to identify the benefits presented by a computerised graphics package when copying and resizing images.

The aims Children are encouraged to experiment with patterns. Emphasis is placed on creativity and the use of a range of methods and tools. Children learn to identify repeating patterns and recognise symmetry through practical activities and by looking at examples in the world of art and design. This relates directly to numeracy learning objectives involving shape and space as well as art and design aspects.

Keywords Pattern, Image, Rotate, Resize, Symmetry

Suggested activities

☞ Produce repeating patterns using potato shapes, buttons, stencils or any other tool that can be used as a stamp. Look at examples of wrapping paper or wallpaper to illustrate.

☞ Repeat the exercise using a graphics program. Some computer packages include stamps; other packages allow the children to draw and colour their own stamp. Demonstrate how to copy and paste the picture (stamp) to produce a repeating pattern. Point out the undo feature and suggest it is used rather than erasing mistakes. Compare the manual and computerised approach to making a repeating pattern.

☞ Discuss the work of Seurat and his use of dots when painting a picture. Access the All Posters website and search for some examples of his work. Copy one of his pictures to a document (right-click on it and save) and using an electronic whiteboard, zoom in so that the children can see how the picture is composed. Using paints, encourage the children to produce a 'pointillist' painting. They can then recreate their painting using a graphics package such as MS Paintbrush or the Textease CT paint palette. Demonstrate how to alter the size and pattern of the brush tool to produce a 'pointillist' effect.

☞ Use a computer graphics program to manipulate repeated images by using the copying, rotating and resizing facilities. Demonstrate how to use these tools and then provide a suitable activity such as drawing a fish and then copying, resizing and rotating the images to produce a fish tank.

4C – Branching databases

What's it all about? This unit extends questioning techniques by using more focused closed questions (yes/no response) to sort and classify. By using branching databases, children can visualise the process required to classify objects based on given criteria (see Chapter 6).

The aims Children are encouraged to identify objects based on the answers to yes/no questions: is it 2-D, is it 3-D, does it have 4 sides? By drawing up a simple branching database they can visualise the route taken to make the identification. This unit has strong links to numeracy.

Keywords Tree diagram/Binary tree, Branching database, Database, Search, Sort

Suggested activities

☞ Recap on the principles by repeating some of the suggested activities from Unit 2E. Make the activities more difficult by having a selection of ten or more different objects and encourage the children to ask questions that will result in early identification of the chosen object (will eliminate several of the items in one go).

☞ Introduce the tree diagram as a visual representation of the selection process. Working with a selection of 2-D and 3-D shapes, allow the children to identify a shape through questioning. Create a Tree diagram to represent the process. Repeat this activity using a number of different data sets (access the G2fL website for lesson plans and picture cards that can be used during activities, select Site map, Teachers, ICT, Resources, Greenwich ICT lesson plans and support files, Unit 4C).

☞ Reinforce the activities by using a computerised branching database package (see Chapter 6).

4D – Collecting and presenting information

What's it all about? This unit is designed to provide experience of collecting and presenting information in the most appropriate way. The children are shown how to collect data so that it can be organised logically and easily. They look at methods of entering the data so that it is in an appropriate format for presentation. Throughout, they are encouraged to consider clarity and accuracy.

The aims Children are shown how to collect information and record the results accurately and clearly. This includes structuring and designing simple questionnaires, designing a database structure and recording the results as a database. Children are shown a variety of methods of presenting the data including bar charts, pie charts and line graphs. This unit can easily be integrated into subject areas such as mathematics, geography and science.

Keywords Graph/Chart, Data/Information, Database, Questionnaire

Suggested activities

☞ Show the children a range of graphs (bar, line and pie) and compare the information they provide. Use graphs as a means of representing data at every opportunity particularly during science activities.

☞ Discuss data collection, emphasising the importance of accuracy. Using a suitable example from a cross-curricular topic, show the children how to use a computer program to create a graph. There are numerous topics that can be chosen for this activity but it is important to make sure that the data can be meaningfully represented as a pie, bar and line chart. As an example, collect data on the weather:

- ❑ Collect data for seven records (days).
- ❑ Include fields such as day, temp. at 9 a.m., temp. at midday, temp. at 3 p.m., weather (sunny/cloudy/raining).
- ❑ Create a computer-based database to hold the information.
- ❑ Design the questionnaire/data collection form to mirror the database structure.
- ❑ Collect the data and enter it into the database.
- ❑ Create appropriate graphs to represent the data.

4E – Modelling effects on screen

What's it all about?   This unit is designed to introduce children to computer programming. Following on from earlier units involving the giving and receiving of instructions, this unit considers providing instructions to control the movement of a robot or turtle around a screen.

The aims   Through practical activities the children learn a simple programming language with commands to control movement. They learn to write a simple procedure that can be repeated and modified based on the required outcome (see Chapter 8).

Keywords   Program, Instructions/Commands, Procedure, Repeat

Suggested activities

Refer to the DfES Standards site for examples; select Unit 4E.

☞   Recap on the learning points from Unit 2D and demonstrate a floor robot or turtle. Allow the children to re-familiarise themselves with programming the toy. Introduce a screen robot/turtle program and recognise that the same language is used to program both a screen and floor turtle; however, point out that the size of numbers used for distance is different.

☞   Show the children how to use the 'Logo' programming language to move the turtle around the screen. Help them to produce two shapes on the screen and show them how to move the screen robot/turtle without drawing a line.

☞   Introduce the repeat instruction to carry out a sequence a defined number of times and show the children that sequences of instructions can be given names and edited (procedures). Look at combining procedures to carry out a more complex set of instructions.

Year 5

Year 5 is a full-on year when it comes to ICT. The QCA scheme of work includes six units. Some of these units develop skills established in previous years and others introduce new ICT concepts such as spreadsheets, control software and datalogging. The Year 5 teacher has a difficult task integrating all these new ICT skills into the curriculum, mainly due to time constraints rather than lack of opportunity. However, with some careful planning and a little application it can be successfully achieved.

Benchmarking

Year 4 allowed time for consolidation of ICT skills particularly in the areas of word-processed documentation and graphical representation of data.

Expectations for pupils entering Year 5

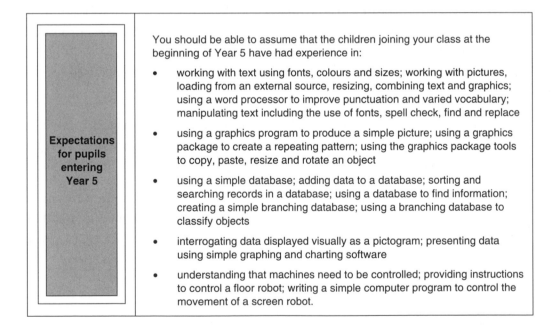

Expectations for pupils entering Year 5

You should be able to assume that the children joining your class at the beginning of Year 5 have had experience in:

- working with text using fonts, colours and sizes; working with pictures, loading from an external source, resizing, combining text and graphics; using a word processor to improve punctuation and varied vocabulary; manipulating text including the use of fonts, spell check, find and replace

- using a graphics program to produce a simple picture; using a graphics package to create a repeating pattern; using the graphics package tools to copy, paste, resize and rotate an object

- using a simple database; adding data to a database; sorting and searching records in a database; using a database to find information; creating a simple branching database; using a branching database to classify objects

- interrogating data displayed visually as a pictogram; presenting data using simple graphing and charting software

- understanding that machines need to be controlled; providing instructions to control a floor robot; writing a simple computer program to control the movement of a screen robot.

ACTIVITY

You may choose to carry out a number of simple activities at the beginning of the year to check or assess this knowledge and expertise. It is suggested that you do this adapting a few of the more general tasks carried out in previous years or by designing an integrated activity to encompass a range of skills. Make a note of individual abilities on a spreadsheet or similar and keep a record of progress throughout the year.

ICT skills

Developing ICT skills in Year 5

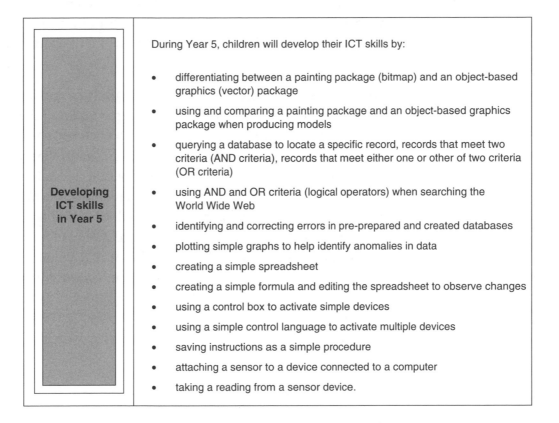

Developing ICT skills in Year 5

During Year 5, children will develop their ICT skills by:

- differentiating between a painting package (bitmap) and an object-based graphics (vector) package

- using and comparing a painting package and an object-based graphics package when producing models

- querying a database to locate a specific record, records that meet two criteria (AND criteria), records that meet either one or other of two criteria (OR criteria)

- using AND and OR criteria (logical operators) when searching the World Wide Web

- identifying and correcting errors in pre-prepared and created databases

- plotting simple graphs to help identify anomalies in data

- creating a simple spreadsheet

- creating a simple formula and editing the spreadsheet to observe changes

- using a control box to activate simple devices

- using a simple control language to activate multiple devices

- saving instructions as a simple procedure

- attaching a sensor to a device connected to a computer

- taking a reading from a sensor device.

Suggestions for ways to integrate ICT into the Year 5 curriculum

Due to the sheer volume of learning objectives it is vital that the Year 5 teacher finds innovative ways to integrate the development of ICT skills within cross-curricular applications. The following sections provide an overview for each Year 5 QCA unit with suggestions on how to develop ICT skills 'on the job'.

5A – Graphical modelling

 What's it all about?　This unit is designed to demonstrate the differences between a paint program (stores images as bitmaps) and an object-based graphics program (stores images as objects); see Chapter 7 for further details.

The aims　Children are encouraged to use a painting package and an object-based graphics package to carry out the same task and then compare the benefits and disadvantages of each package. The children discover that the object-based graphics program has definite advantages when creating images and visual models such as plans, collages and similar artwork that requires the manipulation of objects to achieve a specific aim. Objects can be placed on top of each other (layered), rotated, resized and easily positioned and repositioned to create the finished model. The painting program is less suitable for this kind of task but has benefits for artistic projects; each dot (pixel) can be manipulated separately allowing the production of accurate and professional images. The topics covered in this unit can easily be integrated into art and design sessions.

 Keywords　Object, Pixel, Layer, Manipulate

Suggested activities

☞　Demonstrate a drawing/painting package and an object-based graphics package, pointing out differences between the two. See Chapter 7 for details on the differences between these types of graphics software.

☞　Create a still-life painting using traditional methods and reproduce the artwork using a painting package and an object-based graphics package. Discuss advantages and disadvantages of all three design methods.

☞　Produce a collage using a range of materials and then introduce the use of a painting package and an object-based graphics package for the same task. Discuss advantages and disadvantages of all three design methods.

5B – Analysing data and asking questions: using complex searches

What's it all about? This unit builds on the database skills developed in earlier years. The unit introduces the idea that data can be searched using more than one variable. A variety of pre-prepared databases are required for demonstration purposes as well as access to the Internet for searches of the World Wide Web.

The aims Children are shown how to search a database effectively by using a range of logical operators. For example, rather than finding children 'AGE=10', they are shown how to find 'AGE<10' or 'AGE>10', those children younger than 10 or those children older than 10. This is extended to searching based on two criteria, for example to find children 'AGE=10 AND HAIR=Brown'. The program will only return those records where the child is 10 years old and has brown hair. Finally, they look at search criteria that return a record if one or the other of two criteria are met, for example 'HAIR=Brown OR HAIR=Black', to find those children with either brown or black hair. This unit has direct links to numeracy and the use of logical operators and reinforces the related language for the symbols =, >, <.

Keywords Search, Query, Criteria, Inclusive/Exclusive, AND/OR Operator

Suggested activities

☞ Start by recapping on the structure of a database. Using an electronic whiteboard, demonstrate a simple database, pointing out the records and fields. Remind the children how to select a specific record using the = operator and recap on how to sort the database based on a specified criteria.

☞ Use the >, <, => and =< operator when querying a database. Make sure that the children are confident with terms greater than or equal to and less than or equal to. Compare > and < and introduce the terms exclusive and inclusive as appropriate.

☞ Use the AND operator and the OR operator when searching for data. Use examples to illustrate the difference between the two.

☞ Demonstrate the use of operators when searching the World Wide Web. See Chapter 4 for examples.

5C – Evaluating information, checking accuracy and questioning plausibility

What's it all about? This unit is designed to show, by example, the importance of checking information for accuracy. This involves evaluating information for plausibility and anomalies as well as checking for typing and inputting errors. Children are taught to question information and not simply take it at face value.

The aims As part of the learning process children actively collect and assimilate information throughout their school life and beyond. The ability to intuitively recognise when something is wrong is a vital skill to possess; with so much information available through the Internet and more traditional sources it is important to be able to recognise anomalies and information that is implausible. They also need to appreciate that some information is biased and recognise it as such. This unit aims to start to develop those skills by looking at data critically. It integrates with the data-handling skills that form part of the National Numeracy Strategy at Year 5.

Keywords Accuracy, Bias, Anomaly, Plausible/Implausible

Suggested activities

☞ Discuss the use of databases in the real world: the school database containing details of all the children attending the school (name, address, contact telephone number, etc.); hospital databases with details of patients; vehicle database listing registered cars, their number plate and owner. Discuss the implications if there are mistakes with the data.

☞ Produce a database that contains incorrect and implausible data. For example, misspelt names, incorrect entries in logical fields and implausible numerical data such as a person's height being 1500 cm. Encourage the children to check the data and point out errors. Discuss the importance of not taking it for granted that data is correct; it is not uncommon for someone entering data to make a mistake.

☞ Demonstrate how to check for anomalies using graphical output. Produce a database that logs temperature over a period of time. Enter one temperature reading that is inconsistent with the rest of the data. Plot the data and show the children how the anomaly is apparent from the graph (point out that the data may not be wrong but that data entry should be double checked). Produce another database containing an anomaly and help the children to plot the appropriate data.

5D – Introduction to spreadsheets

What's it all about?   This unit is designed to introduce spreadsheet software and the benefits it can bring when calculating totals. Children are shown how to add labels and data to a spreadsheet and how to create a simple formula to calculate column and row totals (see Chapter 6).

The aims   Through practical applications children are shown how to create and modify a simple spreadsheet. This includes adding labels and data, creating simple formula using cell addresses, using the SUM function, modifying data and checking results. This skill can be developed through the use of spreadsheets in cross curricular activities particularly mathematics and science.

Keywords   Spreadsheet, Cell, Formula, Function

Suggested activities

☞   Produce a simple costing model on paper; discuss the content with the children, explaining how you have added up the numbers in each column/row manually/with a calculator. Consider making changes to the data; what will this involve? Discuss the difficulties of making changes to a paper-based document.

☞   Demonstrate spreadsheet basics; show the children how to add labels and data to the sheet. Allow time for them to experiment with entering information into cells and, when confident, recreate the paper-based model (without the totals).

☞   Demonstrate how to create a simple formula using cell addresses, =C5+C6+C7. Encourage the children to complete the model by adding formulae in the relevant cells. Show the children how easy it is to make changes to the data and observe how the totals automatically update.

☞   Throughout the year, include the use of simple spreadsheets whenever appropriate. As confidence grows introduce the use of the SUM function to add columns and rows of data.

5E – Controlling devices

What's it all about? This unit develops the skills previously gained through considering the importance of instructions when controlling devices. Children are shown how to control simple devices such as buzzers, lights and small motors. Initially providing instructions to turn the device on and off, the children progress to devising a sequence of instructions to carry out a predefined task (see Chapter 8).

The aims This activity involves the children using (or being shown at the very least) a control box that can activate simple output devices. Simulation activities are ideal for reinforcement but there is no substitute for the 'real thing'.

Keywords Control, Device, Output, Program, Flowchart

Suggested activities

Refer to the DfES Standards site for examples; select Unit 5E.

☞ Consider a range of devices/machines that the children come across on a daily basis. Discuss how they operate; is it through a single instruction (on/off) or through a sequence of instructions? A lift or barrier provides an example of control through a single instruction: a pressure pad senses a car approaching and the barrier rises; the press of a button sends the lift to a specific floor. A pelican crossing provides an example of a device that works by a sequence of controls. Consider roles that can be carried out by a machine or a person (a pelican crossing or a lollipop man/woman); what are the advantages, disadvantages?

☞ Introduce a control box and show the children how to plug a light bulb into the first output socket. Remind the children of the control language they used in Year 4 to control the movements of a screen turtle. Recap on the importance of accuracy and precision when writing a program and the benefits of using procedures for repetitive tasks. Show the children how to control the operation of the light bulb. Write a procedure to make the bulb flash on and off; give the procedure a meaningful name.

☞ Write a sequence of instructions to carry out a recognisable event such as the traffic light sequence or the sequence of disco lights. Extend the traffic light program to consider the sequence of events when operating a pelican crossing.

☞ Consider the consequences when the instructions provided are wrong. Write a program to control a device such as a heater. Turn the heater on in the morning, off during the day, on again for the evening and off at bedtime.

5F – Monitoring environmental conditions and changes

What's it all about? This unit is designed to demonstrate that a sensor device attached to a computer can be used to monitor and measure environmental conditions such as changes in temperature, noise, or movement. This is known as computerised datalogging and has some obvious advantages over manual datalogging when it comes to taking readings over long time periods or in areas where there are adverse weather conditions (see Chapter 6).

The aims Through activities the children learn to appreciate the advantages of automated datalogging. By recording changes over a 24-hour period they understand that computerised datalogging is more convenient than manually taking hourly readings. They also consider taking readings from inhospitable or inaccessible regions such as the moon, the Arctic or deep within a tropical rainforest.

Suggested activities

☞ Discuss the problems that may be encountered when collecting data; concentrate on examples involving measurement of environmental data such as temperature, weather conditions or noise. Consider examples of collecting data on the weather conditions in the Arctic or deep within the rainforest, measuring the noise of tremor strength during an earthquake or the eruption of a volcano. Bring the discussion back to more relevant examples such as measuring the temperature in the school over a 24-hour period or measuring fluctuations in noise or light in a certain part of the school over a prolonged period.

☞ Demonstrate how a sensor can be attached to a computer to take readings of conditions such as light intensity, temperature and sound levels. Allow the opportunity for the children to experiment with the equipment.

☞ Carry out some datalogging experiments. For example, log the temperatures over a period of time of a series of beakers insulated with different materials (see the Keeping warm activity at the DCP Microdevelopments website). Fill each beaker with water of a set temperature and measure the cooling of the water. Alternatively, log the changes of light, sound or temperature over a 24-hour period.

Year 6

Year 6 teachers have the added pressure of preparing children for statutory or internal tests and the transition to high school. This makes it all the more difficult to find time to teach the ICT skills outlined in the QCA scheme of work for this year group. To reflect this there are only four ICT units in Year 6 and although substantial in content they all expand on topics covered in previous years. With some careful planning it is possible to build some elements of ICT into the Standard Assessment Tests (SATs) preparation (or revision) timetable, with time being allocated after the tests for an end-of-year project that is ICT driven.

Benchmarking

By the time children reach Year 6 they should have a thorough grounding in the full range of ICT areas included within the ICT primary curriculum. Year 6 provides the opportunity to extend their experience by looking at further application of ICT. By this stage they should confidently use the full range of software listed at the beginning of this part and actively look to use ICT as a tool for cross-curricular activities.

ACTIVITY

In order to benchmark the children's experience and knowledge at this stage, look back over the previous sections from Year 3 to Year 5 and pull out a selection of activities that cover a range of skills. Adapt these activities so that they have relevance to current Year 6 topics. Make a note of the current ability of the children and identify areas that need reinforcement.

ICT skills

Developing ICT skills in Year 6

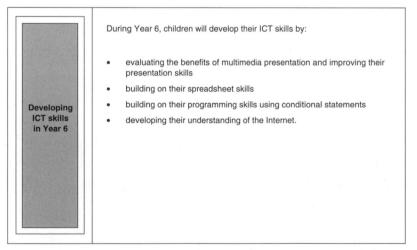

During Year 6, children will develop their ICT skills by:

- evaluating the benefits of multimedia presentation and improving their presentation skills
- building on their spreadsheet skills
- building on their programming skills using conditional statements
- developing their understanding of the Internet.

Suggestions for ways to integrate ICT into the Year 6 curriculum

The four ICT units for Year 6 can be consolidated into the general curriculum or treated as mini projects. Unit 6B can easily be integrated within science topics with Units 6A and 6D being embedded throughout the year or included as projects for the 'after SATs/internal tests' period at the end of the year. Unit 6C can be covered as an external activity if facilities such as a City Learning Centre or suitably equipped High School are available.

6A – Multimedia presentation

What's it all about?
This unit is designed to encourage children to consider multi-meadia when designing and developing a presentation. They create a presentation using text, sounds and pictures and learn how to use hyperlinks to connect interrelated pages.

The aims
This unit provides a creative challenge, bringing together materials and information generated across the curriculum. Graphics and pictures can be created during art and design sessions. Sounds, or more specifically music, can be created during music sessions and the content for the presentation can be developed within any discipline. The aim is to bring these elements together using a multimedia presentation package such as MS PowerPoint.

This activity can be integrated into a suitable curriculum topic such as history or geography or can form an independent project. The aim is to:

- discuss the benefits of multimedia over other means of communication

- look at multimedia information

- consider website design and what constitutes a good web page

- produce a flowchart of a website or presentation

- produce a multimedia presentation that includes sound, text and pictures.

Suggested activities

☞ There is a host of examples of suitable projects, one being the design of a school website and a presentation outlining the process involved (note, this does not involve producing the website; just designing the look, feel, researching and writing the content and producing a flowchart of the pages and links).

6B – Spreadsheet modelling

What's it all about? This unit builds on the spreadsheet skills developed during Year 5. By building both mathematical and scientific models, the children learn to create appropriate formulae. They also use the models to experiment with 'What if … ?' scenarios by changing data and predicting results.

The aims The aim of this unit is to develop skills and increase the knowledge of the functionality of a spreadsheet package. The children learn to copy text, values and formulas, how to create more complex formulas and how to generate a graph from the data. Emphasis is placed on accuracy and checking the plausibility of the data. This unit can be meaningfully integrated into Year 6 science tasks.

Suggested activities

☞ Remind the children how spreadsheet formulae are created (C6+C7, C7/C3, C5–C4, C2*C6, SUM(C1:C6), etc. Reinforce using some simple activities (this could form part of the benchmarking tasks at the beginning of the year).

☞ The ICT aim for this unit is to show the children how to copy formulae, use the data in the spreadsheet to draw a graph and query the data by asking 'What if … ?' questions. All of these skills can be directly applied to the science activities carried out during Year 6.

6C – Control and monitoring – What happens when ...?

What's it all about? This unit builds on the skills introduced and developed in Year 5 where children learned how to control a device such as a buzzer or light by switching it on and off. In this unit the process is extended to programming the computer to carry out a process when it detects change (see Chapter 8).

The aims Children are shown how to attach devices such as pressure pads, light sensors, magnetic switches, on/off switches or other devices to a control box. The aim is to then program the computer to carry out a specific process when it detects some sort of change, for example switch on the light when it gets dark. This involves learning some new commands such as 'if ... then' which are needed to program the control box to make such decisions.

Suggested activities

Refer to the DfES Standards site for examples; select Unit 6C.

☞ Discuss the range of devices that monitor physical changes in the environment. Explain that they usually rely on a sensor that is specifically designed to react to a particular type of change such as temperature, movement, light, sound or pressure. For example, street lights come on when it gets dark or central heating comes on when the temperature drops.

☞ Discuss the difference between an output and input device (input feeds information into the computer – switch, sensor, etc.; output is controlled by the computer – buzzer, bulb, motor, etc.). Discuss cause and effect.

☞ Consider a simple task such as turning on a light when a switch is pressed. Produce a flowchart before writing the program. Test the program using a control box. Progress to using two inputs and one output, for example the light comes on if it is after 6 p.m. and it is dark.

☞ Use a control technology simulator to program some 'real life' scenarios such as a house security system, controlling a lighthouse, a theme park, a kitchen with appliances, or pelican crossing.

6D – Using the Internet to search large databases and to interpret information

 What's it all about?

This unit is designed to equip the children with the skills to use complex searches to find data using large databases (such as the Internet). Once they have located information they are taught how to critically appraise the data and recognise fact from personal points of view.

The aims

Through the general use of the Internet, children develop their familiarity with using search engines. Through these activities they practise skim reading and selecting information, appraising information and copying information to other applications (observing copyright). They practise narrowing their searches using a range of keywords and search operators and using hyperlinks to move from site to site. The use of the Favorites option is introduced to save the links to their favourite websites.

Suggested activities

☞ Practise summarising skills away from the computer by encouraging the children to précis articles relating to current areas of the curriculum. This should be carried out throughout the year.

☞ This unit can either be integrated within areas of the curriculum throughout the year and/or included as a project, possibly in the last term, during and after the SATs/internal tests. The project can involve any aspect of the curriculum for Year 6 or it can form part of the presentation task for ICT Unit 6A. From an ICT perspective ensure that the children are comfortable searching the Internet, finding suitable information, copying that information to Word or PowerPoint and using the Favorites feature. To ensure maximum experience, incorporate Internet research wherever possible particularly during history, geography and RE lessons.

End of year assessment

ICT does not currently feature in the formal end of Key Stage 2 SATs tests; however, parents and future high schools will appreciate some indication of progress in this subject. The benchmarking activities at the beginning of the year coupled with ongoing observation throughout Year 6 will provide adequate reference points for a brief report of knowledge and understanding.

Useful websites

All Posters	www.allposters.co.uk
BBC	www.bbc.co.uk/weather/ukweather
Coxhoe Primary School	www.coxhoe.durham.sch.uk/Curriculum/Music.htm
DCP Microdevelopments	www.dcpmicro.com/logit/resources/resources.htm
ePALS	www.epals.com
G2fL Greenwich Grid for Learning	www.lgfl.net/lgfl/leas/greenwich
Inventors	http://inventors.about.com/od/broadcastinghistory/
Kent NGfL	www.kented.org.uk/ngfl/software/simulations
2simple	www.2simple.com
Play Music	www.playmusic.org
Primary Resources	www.primaryresources.co.uk/english
Standards (DfES)	www.standards.dfes.gov.uk/schemes2/it
Tiger Towson	http://tiger.towson.edu/~mlackn1/ILAactivities.htm

Glossaries

Abbreviations

Becta: British Educational Communications and Technology Agency
CAD: **Computer Aided Design**
CC: Carbon Copy
CD: **compact disc**
CD-ROM: **compact disc read-only memory**
CPU: **central processing unit**
DFC: Devolved Formula Capital
DfES: Department for Education and Skills
DVD: **Digital video disc** or **digital versatile disc**
eLC: electronic learning credit
E-mail: **electronic mail**
GUI: graphical user interface
HLTA: Higher Level Teaching Assistant
ICT: **Information and Communication Technology**
INSET: IN SErvice Training
ISBN: International Standard Book Number
ISP: **Internet Service Provider**
IT: **Information Technology**
ITT: Initial Teacher Training
IWB: **interactive whiteboard**
LEA: Local Education Authority
MODEM: **modulator demodulator**
NGfL: National Grid for Learning
NOF: New Opportunities Fund
NQT: Newly Qualified Teacher
NVQ: National Vocational Qualification
OCR: **Optical Character Recognition**
Ofsted: Office for Standards in Education
PC: **personal computer**
PPA: Planning, Preparation and Assessment
QCA: Qualifications and Curriculum Authority
QTS: Qualified Teacher Status
SAT: Standard Assessment Test
TA: Teaching Assistant
TDA: Training and Development Agency

VDU: visual display unit (computer screen)
WWW: **World Wide Web**
URL: **Uniform Resource Locator**

Terms

Broadband:	A high-speed connection to the **Internet** that uses the spare capacity of a telephone line.
Central processing unit (CPU):	The part of the **computer** that processes information. The CPU carries out the vast majority of the calculations performed by a computer. Can be thought of as the brain of a computer.
Chatroom:	A collection of people sending messages to each other, via the **Internet,** in **'real-time'**.
Compact disk (CD):	A removable disc that holds data and **software** that can be copied to and sometimes from the **computer** (a read/write CD).
Computer:	An electronic device used for the storage and processing of information.
Digital:	A method of storing, processing and transmitting information electronically as pulses (represented by the binary digits 0 and 1).
Digital camera:	A camera that stores images electronically rather than on film.
DVD player:	**Digital** video disc (or digital versatile disc) player – used to show films and other visual media that have been stored digitally (on a DVD).
Electronic mail (e-mail):	A method of sending messages, electronically, from one **computer** to another via the **Internet**.
Floppy disk/diskette/disk:	A removable disk that holds data that can be copied to and from the **computer**.
Hard/Fixed disk drive:	A storage device used to store applications (**software**) and data.
Hardware:	**Computer** and computer-related equipment is collectively known as hardware.
Information and Communication Technology (ICT):	The technology used to manage information and aid communication.
Information Technology (IT):	The technology used to manage information.
Inkjet printer:	A printer that sprays ink directly onto the paper through nozzles.

Input device:
A device used to get information into the **computer** such as the keyboard, the **mouse** or a **scanner**.

Install software:
To load **software** onto the **computer** for the first time.

Interactive whiteboard:
An interactive whiteboard is an erasable writing surface that interacts with a **computer** to capture writing electronically and enable interaction with a projected computer image.

Internet:
A worldwide **network** of **computers** that are linked together providing a means of communicating and sharing information.

Internet Service Provider (ISP):
An ISP invests in and manages extensive **computer networks** and provides links to networks across the world. A user needs the services of an ISP to access the **Internet**.

Laptop:
A lightweight, portable, compact **computer** where the **system unit** and **peripherals** are all housed within the same unit.

Laser printer:
A printer that uses a laser to produce an image on a rotating drum. The image is then transferred to paper by using an electric charge to deposit toner.

Modulator demodulator (MODEM):
A device that converts data from **digital** format to analogue and back to digital so that information can travel down a telephone line. Used for 'dial-up' connection to the **Internet**.

Mouse:
A pointing device that aids the input of information into the **computer**; the mouse is used to point to an item/object displayed on the screen which is then selected by clicking the mouse button.

Network:
A computer network is a number of **computers** linked together using cables.

Optical Character Recognition (OCR):
Software that enables the computer to recognise handwriting or printed text and turn it into computer text (digital text) that can be edited.

Output device:
A device used to get information out of the **computer**, such as a printer or speakers.

Peripheral:
A device that is on the perimeter of the **computer** such as a keyboard, **mouse**, printer, **scanner**, speakers or **digital camera** (an add-on).

Real-time:
In a computing context, real-time refers to an occasion where information is received and immediately responded to without any time delay.

Scanner:
A device that converts visual information into **digital** data.

Search engine:	A tool (**software**) used to search the pages of the **WWW** for specific information.
Software:	The program or set of instructions (**computer** application/program) that controls the operation of a computer.
Storage unit/device:	Units that hold information while being processed (internal storage units) or waiting to be processed (external storage units such as a hard **fixed disk** or **removable disk** or **CD** drive).
System unit:	A casing that houses the **central processing unit** and **storage units** of the **computer**.
Upgrade software:	To replace the version or release of the **software** that is currently installed on the **computer** with a more recent or up-to-date version.
Video conferencing:	Two or more people communicating via video link in **'real-time'**.
Video streaming:	Accessing a video file via the Internet in **'real-time'**; playing a file as it is being downloaded.
Virus:	A **computer** virus is a computer program that has been written with the intent of damaging information held on a computer or in extreme cases making the computer unusable.
Web browser:	A tool (**software**) used to navigate the **WWW** such as Microsoft Explorer.
World Wide Web (WWW):	The World Wide Web is made up of billions of linked web pages that contain pictures, text, sounds and animations.
Uniform Resource Locator (**URL**):	The unique address that identifies a website, i.e. www.bbc.co.uk.

Resources

General information

Ask an Expert	www.ictadvice.org.uk/experts
Becta's ICT Advice site	www.ictadvice.org.uk
Becta's schools' website	www.becta.org.uk/schools
Curriculum Online	www.curriculumonline.gov.uk
ICT Advice Website	www.ictadvice.org.uk/primary
National Curriculum online	www.nc.uk.net
National Curriculum Wales	www.new.wales.gov.uk/topics/educationandskills/?lang=en
National Curriculum Scotland	www.ltscotland.org.uk
National Curriculum Northern Ireland	www.ccea.org.uk
NCH	www.nchafc.org.uk
Practice skills tests	www.tda.gov.uk/skillstests/practicematerials.aspx
Professional standards	www.hlta.gov.uk/php/read.php?articleid1385sectionid182
Qualifications and Curriculum Authority	www.qca.org.uk
Scottish Curriculum Framework	www.ltscotland.org.uk
Standards site (DfES)	www.standards.dfes.gov.uk/schemes2/it
Training and Development Agency	www.tda.gov.uk
Teacher Resource Exchange	http://tre.ngfl.gov.uk

Search engines and Internet filters:

AOL   www.aol.com

Ask for Kids   www.askforkids.com

Google   www.google.co.uk

Hotmail   www.hotmail.com

KidsClick!   www.kidsclick.com

Lycos   www.lycos.co.uk

Net Nanny   www.netnanny.com

Yahooligans   www.yahooligans.yahoo.com

Foundation Stage

Curriculum Framework for   www.ltscotland.org.uk
Children 3 to 5

Foundation Profile website   www.qca.org.uk/foundation/

Foundation Stage profile   www.qca.org.uk/163.html
assessment arrangements

Scholastic magazine   www.scholastic.co.uk/magazines/nurseryed.htm

Scottish Curriculum   www.bbc.co.uk/cbeebies/grownups/curriculum/scotland/
Framework for Children
3 to 5

HLTAs

Approved trainers   www.hlta.gov.uk/hltaproviders/

Acceptable qualifications   www.hlta.gov.uk/php/read.php?sectionid179arti-
                               cleid1361

DfES and TTA standards for HLTAs   www.tda.gov.uk/teachers/currentconsultations/
                               professionalstandards/

General information for HLTAs www.hlta.gov.uk

Useful activities and resources

www.abcteach.com/directory/funactivities/mazefun/   Maze activities

www.activityvillage.co.uk/chinesenewyearjigsaws.htm   Jigsaw puzzles

www.allkids.co.uk/kids_pages/early_learning.shtml   Select Kids, free fun sites for a
                                                           range of activities

www.allposters.co.uk	Famous artists – paintings
www.bbc.co.uk/cbeebies	Activities for 3–5 age group
www.bbc.co.uk/schools/magickey/adventures/creamcake.shtml	Wordbank rhyming activity
www.bbc.co.uk/schools/preschool/	Pre-school activities
www.bbc.co.uk/cbeebies/storycircle/fairystories/	Fairy tales
www.bbc.co.uk/weather/ukweather	Weather simulation
www.cogcon.com/gamegoo/gooey.html	Selection of educational games
www.collinseducation.com	HarperCollins ICT Adventure
www.coxhoe.durham.sch.uk/curriculum/music.htm	Music activities
www.dcpmicro.com/logit/resources/resources.htm	Datalogging activities
www.epals.com	Linking schools for email activities
www.fisher-price.com/uk/playtime/	Activities for pre-school
www.fisher-price.com/us/	Select Fun & family time and then choose Fun & games, online! for a range of activities
www.funschool.com	Concentration game, matching pictures
http://inventors.about.com/od/broadcastinghistory/	History of communication
www.hitchams.suffolk.sch.uk/foundation/pixie/index.htm	Floor robot activities
www.hitchams.suffolk.sch.uk/datalogging/examples.htm	Datalogging examples
www.kented.org.uk/ngfl/software/simulations	Simulations
www.kented.org.uk/NGfL/ict/robots/games.htm	Control technology
www.kevinsplayroom.co.uk	Clipart
www.kinderplanet.com/online.htm	Selection of educational activities
www.ladybird.co.uk	Selection of educational activities
www.littlecritter.com	Computer animation
www.longman.com/younglearners/teachers/resources-archive/	Selection of educational activities
www.longman.com/younglearners/students/animals.html	Word bank activity

www.lgfl.net/lgfl/	Select Content, Content grid, ICT for a range of links to resources
www.lgfl.net/lgfl/leas/greenwich	Access the site map and follow the path to Teachers, ICT, Resources and select the Greenwich ICT lesson plans and support files
www.mothergoose.com/GameArcade/onlinegames.htm	Select Monkey music for mouse control practice
www.nelsonthornes.com	Nelson Thornes ICT Handbooks
http://ngfl.northumberland.gov.uk/ict/qca/	Activities for all QCA ICT units
http://ngfl.northumberland.gov.uk/science/databases/default.htm	Branching database activities
www.noddy.com	Educational activities for the early years
www.northerngrid.org/ngflwebsite/cjearlyyears/EarlyYears/ICTearlyyearsskills.htm	Keyboard templates
www.playmusic.org	Music activities
www.primaryresources.co.uk	General ICT resources
www.smart-central.com	Sing-along nursery rhymes and songs
http://sunsite.berkeley.edu/KidsClick21/	Selection of educational activities
www.teachingideas.co.uk/english/contents.htm	ICT and literacy activities
http://tiger.towson.edu/mlackn1/ILAactivities.htm	Selection of educational activities

Software and hardware

2Simple	www.2simple.com
2Investigate	www.2simple.com
Bee-Bot (TTS)	www.beebot.co.uk
BlackCat	www.blackcatsoftware.com
BlackCat Decisions3	www.blackcatsoftware.com/products/decisions3.asp

Commotion Group	www.commotiongroup.co.uk
Data Harvest	www.data-harvest.co.uk
FlexiTREE 2	www.flexible.co.uk/FlexiTREE.html
FlexiCAD	www.flexible.co.uk/FlexiCAD.html
Log-Box (TTS)	www.log-box.co.uk
LogIT Explorer	www.dcpmicro.com/logit/explorer/index.htm
Logotron	www.logo.com
Microsoft	www.microsoft.com
MSWLogo	www.softronix.com/logo.html
RM EasyMail Plus	www.rm.com/easymailplus
Softease	www.softease.com
Swallow Systems	www.swallow.co.uk
Textease Studio CT	www.softease.com
Valiant Technology	www.valiant-technology.com